SEWING WITH SCRAPS

15 Projects to Sew a Sustainable Wardrobe Using Leftover Fabric

BIRGITTA HELMERSSON & SAM GROSE

Photography by Jessica Sidenros & Sam Grose

INTRODUCTION

Do you have an ever-growing collection of fabric scraps from previous sewing projects that you can't bear to throw away but don't actually have a use for? This is a problem that most home sewers face. It's great because it means you don't want to waste fabric – but what exactly can you do with all the scraps?

That question has been at the very heart of Helgrose (our joint business venture) ever since we set up in 2018 after moving our little family from Melbourne, Australia to Malmö, Sweden. Initially, I (Sam) wanted Helgrose to be a unisex workwear-inspired label – just us making clothes in the style we liked. Birgitta, however, had already been running her own label specializing in zero waste pattern cutting for many years and was not at all keen on creating yet another brand piling more textiles into landfill. So we decided we would save every single scrap, both large and small, from our clothing production and repurpose them into items that were functional and appealing, but also relatively efficient to make – not an easy feat, let me tell you!

It forced us to get creative. Some things worked, some things didn't, but eventually we began to find viable ways of utilizing what we had collected. We resurrected Birgitta's grandmother's old loom and, with the help of a talented textile artist friend, made rag rugs from fabric offcuts. Cushions became another great way to use what we had: we created awesomely textured pillowcases, then stuffed them with finely cut textiles and created meditation pillows. We also collaborated with a textile-sorting facility that donated a pallet of unsaleable second-hand jeans, repurposing them into patchwork garments. Over time, we became known for sewing with scraps, using them both to create brand-new garments and to embellish and extend the life of existing ones.

Along the way we've refined our techniques, using them alongside Birgitta's zero waste patterns, and so with this book we want to teach you some of our favourite methods. We've provided detailed step-by-step instructions for a range of unisex clothes and accessories, so that you can copy them yourself – but what we really hope is that you'll be inspired to make fun, functional and wearable garments and accessories of your very own. After all, everyone's scrap basket will contain different things – different fabrics, different colours, different patterns. By sewing with scraps you'll not only be doing your bit for the environment, but you'll also be creating unique pieces that define your personal style – and that's a win-win for everyone!

We hope you enjoy using this book as much as enjoyed writing it!

Birgitta & Sam

2019: OUR DAUGHTER ASTRID HIDING BEHIND A GIANT PILE OF SECOND-HAND DENIM JEANS, DONATED BY A TEXTILE-SORTING FACILITY.

2024: BIRGITTA WEARING A HELGROSE VEST MADE USING COLLAGED FABRIC REMNANTS.

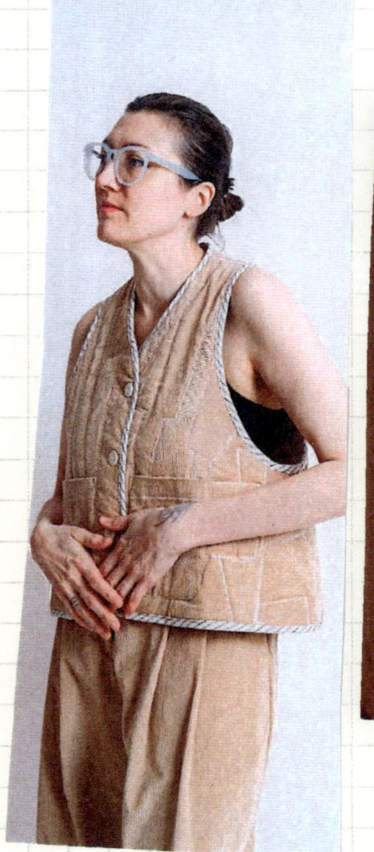

2022: BIRGITTA PLANNING A PATCHWORK GARMENT WITH VINTAGE AND SECOND-HAND FABRICS.

2018: BIRGITTA, SAM AND ASTRID, MOVING TEXTILES AROUND MALMÖ.

2019: THE DAY WE MET OUR FRIEND LUDJERO, WHO IS ALSO A MODEL IN THIS BOOK. HERE HE IS OUTSIDE THE FRONT OF OUR SHOP WEARING THE HELGROSE STATION SHIRT.

2021: ANTI BIRGITTA'S BROTHER-IN-LAW, WHO IS ALSO A MODEL IN THIS BOOK. HERE ANTI IS PICTURED WEARING A HELGROSE TWINSET MADE USING VINTAGE FABRICS, HOLDING OUR DAUGHTER AILA IN OUR BACKYARD.

2018: A BEDSPREAD AND TWO RUGS IN OUR HOME, MADE USING REPURPOSED TEXTILES.

2020: AILA ASLEEP ON A BED OF FABRIC SCRAPS.

2021: HELGROSE WORKWEAR JACKET MADE USING VINTAGE AND SECOND-HAND FABRICS.

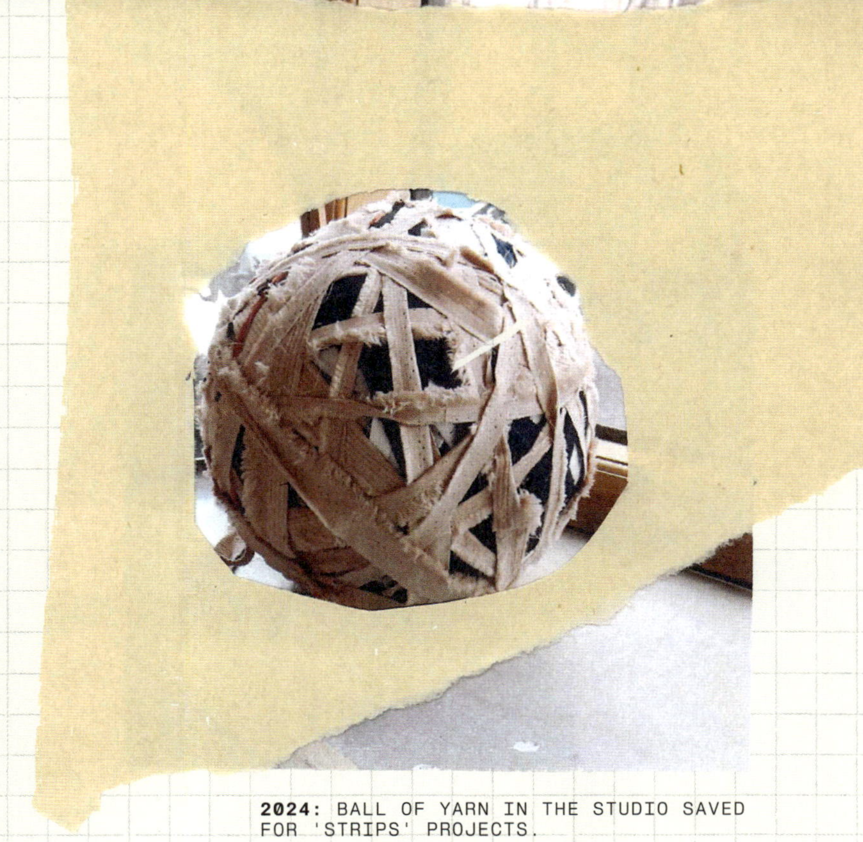

2024: BALL OF YARN IN THE STUDIO SAVED FOR 'STRIPS' PROJECTS.

2021: HELGROSE PATCHWORK OVERALLS MADE USING VINTAGE AND SECOND-HAND FABRICS.

2018: 'COMMUNITY LOOM' FOR PASSERS-BY TO ADD TO USING REPURPOSED TEXTILES.

2019: PATTERNS HANGING IN OUR STUDIO.

2019: STUDIO ASSISTANT GABIJA WEARING A QUILTED JACKET MADE FROM DONATED SECOND-HAND JEANS.

2021: FABRICS, DYED BY SAM USING FOOD SCRAPS, DRYING IN OUR BACKYARD.

2019: SAM MAKING A RAG RUG USING REPURPOSED STUDIO SCRAPS ON BIRGITTA'S GRANDMOTHER'S LOOM.

HOW TO USE

This is a book of ideas to inspire you to use scraps in creative ways to make functional and wearable garments, plus some fun accessories.

It includes three different core methods – patchwork, strips and collage – and 15 projects using these methods. You can scan the QR code and download three of our favourite and most popular Helgrose patterns to get you started – the Workwear Jacket, Comfort Pants and Tee (sizes XS–6XL) – and use them in the projects or try the methods out with some of your own patterns. Just have fun, test out new ideas and see where it leads you!

THIS BOOK

METHODS + PROJECTS

Each chapter introduces a particular way of working with fabric scraps and is followed by a selection of projects. The methods and projects included in this book are:

PATCHWORK (PAGES 44–103)

This is possibly the most well-known method of using scraps. We take you through how to plan and prepare your patchwork, as well as different seam techniques and ideas to inspire you to use patchwork in creative ways. This chapter includes six projects to inspire you to test out your new skills – a classic workwear jacket, a long quilted coat, a playful and colourful patchwork tee, a re-make denim jacket, comfort pants and short shorts.

STRIPS (PAGES 104–145)

This method is based on making fabric yarn from leftover fabrics, so essentially cutting the fabric into strips and attaching them to a base fabric to add structure and decoration. Strips can be used in several different creative ways and create beautiful texture. This chapter includes four projects: a roomy textural tote bag, a bowler shirt, a decorative plaid jacket and a skirt with a lush and fluffy border detail.

COLLAGE (PAGES 146–187)

Making collage with fabric is super fun! This method is based on the technique of appliqué but we wanted a broader term as there are so many fun variations of this technique you can do, and the name 'collage' seemed to fit the bill! In this method we take you through several ideas of using fabric collage to inspire you to experiment with all sorts of different scraps. This chapter includes five projects: a tone-on-tone trans-season vest, an appliqué t-shirt, a collage 'print' jumper re-make, a denim jeans re-make, and (one of our faves from the book) a terrazzo clutch bag.

SKILL LEVELS

Each project has been given a skill level. Levels 1–2 are suitable for beginners, level 3 is for confident beginners, and levels 4–5 are for intermediate to experienced sewers.

PATTERNS

The three patterns available to download with this book are used in various ways throughout the projects and are some of our most-loved Helgrose styles from the last few years. Each one is a great addition to your wardrobe, both wearable and comfortable.

As we have used the patterns in different ways, the fabric estimates and ways of cutting the pieces out vary greatly in different projects. Refer to each individual project for more info. If you want to use the patterns as they are, using fabric off the roll, we have provided some basic estimates of fabric usage by size in the pages that follow, allowing for some extra. Please keep in mind that these can vary if you are making other variations of these patterns.

The patterns are:

- Workwear Jacket
- Comfort Pants
- Tee

To access the patterns, please scan the QR code below and download them onto your device. They can then be printed out and assembled.

COMFORT PANTS

WORKWEAR JACKET

TEE

WORKWEAR JACKET: SIZES XS/S–5XL/6XL

A versatile design with a relaxed fit. The main pattern is a classic workwear shape with patch pockets and a collar. The pattern features additional pattern pieces to modify the design into a short-sleeved bowler shirt (Swirl Shirt) and a long coat (Quilted Coat). To see which pattern size to select, see page 18.

WORKWEAR JACKET PATTERN PIECES

- A: Front body
- B: Back body
- C: Workwear sleeve
- D: Front facing
- E: Back facing
- F: Workwear collar
- G: Sleeve cuff
- H: Sleeve split binding
- I: Chest pocket
- J: Hip pockets
- K: Neck loop

ADDITIONAL PATTERN PIECES FOR THE SWIRL SHIRT AND QUILTED COAT

- L: Bowler collar
- M: Coat collar
- N: Front lining
- O: Back lining
- P: Coat sleeve (outer/lining)
- Q: Pocket welt
- R: Pocket facing
- S: Pocket underlining
- T: Pocket top lining

The cutting layouts and changes required for the variations are shown in the individual project instructions.

FABRIC ESTIMATES

These estimates are based on using the main Workwear Jacket style in a fabric that is 145 cm (57 in.) wide, as shown in the layout plans:

<u>XS/S–M/L</u>

1.75 m (1⅞ yd)

<u>L/XL–3XL/4XL</u>

2.15 m (2⅜ yd)

<u>4XL/5XL–5XL/6XL</u>

2.4 m (2⅝ yd)

NOTIONS

Based on using the main Workwear Jacket pattern as shown in the cutting layouts.

	XS/S	S/M	M/L	L/XL	XL/2XL	2XL/3XL	3XL/4XL	4XL/5XL	5XL/6XL
BIAS BINDING: 4 CM (1½ IN.) WIDE, IN A LIGHT-WEIGHT COTTON	290 cm (114 in.)	300 cm (118 in.)	310 cm (122 in.)	320 cm (126 in.)	330 cm (130 in.)	340 cm (134 in.)	350 cm (138 in.)	360 cm (142 in.)	370 cm (146 in.)
IRON-ON INTERFACING MEDIUM-WEIGHT	FOR FRONT FACINGS (D), BACK FACING (E), AND ONE COLLAR PIECE (F) All sizes: Approx. 60 x 115 cm (24 x 46 in.)								
BUTTONS	FOR FRONT AND SLEEVE CUFFS All sizes: six, each 25 mm (1 in.)								

LAYOUT PLANS

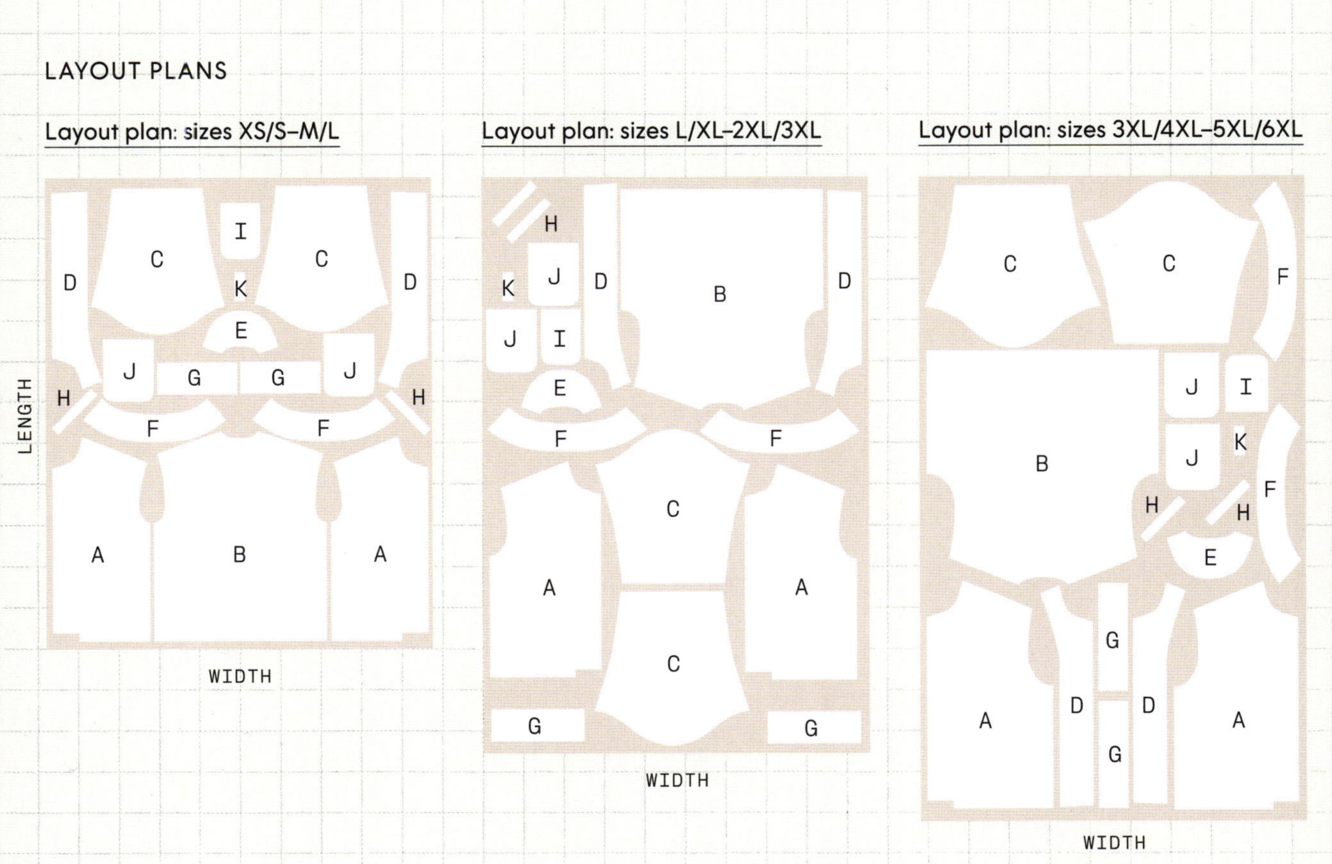

COMFORT PANTS: XS–6XL

Our most popular pants to date, these feature welt pockets, front pleats and an elasticated waist for a classic, tailored look that is still ultra comfortable and wearable. This pattern also includes a shorts version; refer to the Short Shorts instructions (page 64) for the changes required. To see which pattern size to select, see page 19.

PATTERN PIECES

- A: Front leg
- B: Back leg
- C: Waistband
- D: Pocket welt
- E: Front pocket facing
- F: Front pocket lining
- G: Back pocket facing
- H: Back pocket lining

FABRIC ESTIMATES

Based on using fabric that is 145 cm (57 in.) wide, as shown in the layout plans:

XS–M:

1.65 m (1⅞ yd)

L–2XL:

1.9 m (2⅛ yd)

3XL–6XL:

2.5 m (2¾ yd)

NOTIONS

	XS	S	M	L	XL	2XL	3XL	4XL	5XL	6XL
ELASTIC: 5 CM (2 IN.) WIDE	70 cm (27½ in.)	75 cm (29½ in.)	80 cm (31½ in.)	85 cm (33½ in.)	90 cm (35½ in.)	90 cm (35½ in.)	100 cm (39½ in.)	105 cm (41½ in.)	110 cm (43½ in.)	115 cm (45½ in.)
BIAS BINDING: 4 CM (1½ IN.) WIDE, IN A LIGHT-WEIGHT COTTON	165 cm (65 in.)	170 cm (67 in.)	175 cm (69 in.)	180 cm (71 in.)	185 cm (73 in.)	190 cm (75 in.)	195 cm (77 in.)	200 cm (79 in.)	205 cm (81 in.)	210 cm (83 in.)
IRON-ON INTERFACING MEDIUM-WEIGHT	FOR POCKET WELT (D) PIECES All sizes: 25 x 20 cm (10 x 8 in.)									

LAYOUT PLANS

Layout plan: sizes XS–M

LENGTH

WIDTH

Layout plan: sizes L–2XL

WIDTH

Layout plan: sizes 3XL–6XL

WIDTH

TEE: XS/S–5XL/6XL

This is a classic unisex tee that has a relaxed fit with a crew neck and a ribbing neckband. This pattern also incorporates an option to make a vest/waistcoat, with a slightly different shoulder and armhole shape, and a centre front seam with rouleau ties to close; refer to the Piece Vest instructions (pages 177–178) for the layout plans and changes required. To see which pattern size to select, see page 19.

PATTERN PIECES

- A: Front
- B: Back
- C: Sleeve
- D: Neckband

FABRIC ESTIMATES

Based on using fabric that is 145 cm (57 in.) wide, as shown in the layout plans:

Cotton jersey (pieces A, B and C)

XS/S–2XL/3XL:

1.2 m (1⅜ yd)

3XL/4XL–5XL/6XL:

1.8 m (2 yd)

Cotton 2 x 1 ribbing (piece D)

XS/S–2XL/3XL:

Approx. 46 x 6 cm (18 x 2½ in.)

3XL/4XL–5XL/6XL:

Approx. 52 x 6 cm (21 x 2½ in.)

LAYOUT PLANS

Layout plan: sizes XS/S–2XL/3XL

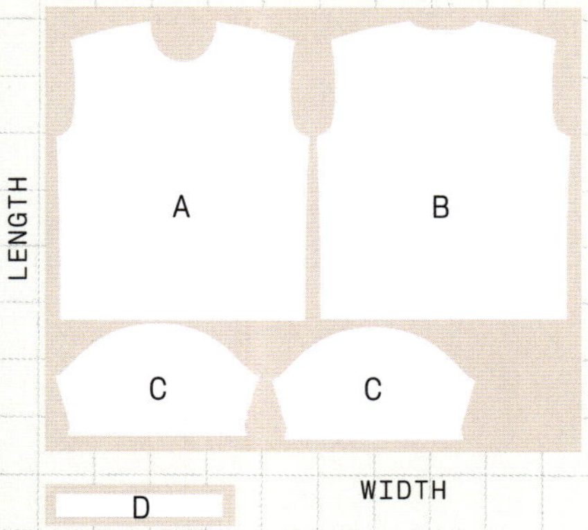

LENGTH

A

B

C

C

D

WIDTH

Layout plan: sizes 3XL/4XL–5XL/6XL

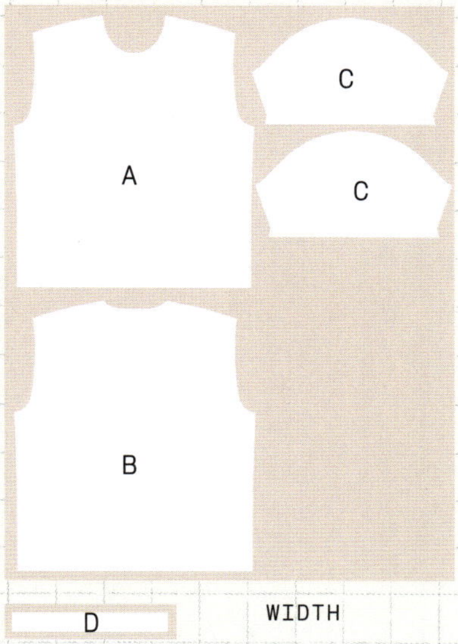

A

C

C

B

D

WIDTH

CHOOSING YOUR SIZE

The patterns in this book use two sizing structures: XS/S–5XL/6XL and XS–6XL. Refer to these charts to help you choose your size for each pattern. The measurements allow for around 15 cm (6 in.) ease in the chest and hip measurements.

WORKWEAR JACKET

	XS/S	S/M	M/L	L/XL	XL/2XL	2XL/3XL	3XL/4XL	4XL/5XL	5XL/6XL
CHEST/HIP	90.5 cm (35½ in.)	98 cm (38½ in.)	105.5 cm (41½ in.)	113 cm (44½ in.)	120.5 cm (47½ in.)	128 cm (50½ in.)	135.5 cm (53½ in.)	143 cm (56¼ in.)	150.5 cm (59¼ in.)
BODY LENGTH*	68 cm (26¾ in.)	69.5 cm (27⅜ in.)	71 cm (28 in.)	72.5 cm (28½ in.)	74 cm (29 in.)	75.5 cm (29¾ in.)	77 cm (30½ in.)	78.5 cm (31 in.)	80 cm (31½ in.)
SLEEVE LENGTH*	77 cm (30½ in.)	78.5 cm (31 in.)	80 cm (31½ in.)	81.5 cm (32 in.)	83 cm (32½ in.)	84.5 cm (33¼ in.)	86 cm (34 in.)	87.5 cm (34½ in.)	89 cm (35 in.)

*The body length is measured from shoulder to hem. The sleeve length is measured on the Workwear Jacket sleeve from neck to finished hem, as the sleeve has a dropped shoulder. The Quilted Coat sleeve is 2.5 cm (1 in.) shorter than the Workwear Jacket sleeve.

COMFORT PANTS

	XS	S	M	L	XL	2XL	3XL	5XL	6XL
WAIST*	65–70 cm (25½–27½ in.)	70–75 cm (27½–29½ in.)	75–80 cm (29½–31½ in.)	80–85 cm (31½–33½ in.)	85–90 cm (33½–35½ in.)	90–95 cm (35½–37½ in.)	95–100 cm (37½–39½ in.)	105–110 cm (41½–43½ in.)	110–115 cm (43½–45¼ in.)
HIP	89 cm (35 in.)	94 cm (37 in.)	99 cm (39 in.)	104 cm (41 in.)	110 cm (43½ in.)	117 cm (46 in.)	125 cm (49¼ in.)	141 cm (55½ in.)	150 cm (59 in.)
LENGTH*	101.5 cm (40 in.)	103 cm (40½ in.)	104.5 cm (41 in.)	106 cm (41¾ in.)	107.5 cm (42 in.)	109 cm (43 in.)	110.5 cm (43½ in.)	113.5 cm (44¾ in.)	115 cm (45¼ in.)
INSIDE LEG	72 cm (28⅜ in.)	73.5 cm (29 in.)	75 cm (29½ in.)	76.5 cm (30 in.)	78 cm (30¾ in.)	79.5 cm (31¼ in.)	81 cm (31¾ in.)	84 cm (33 in.)	85.5 cm (33½ in.)
CROTCH*	74 cm (29 in.)	75.5 cm (29¾ in.)	77 cm (30⅜ in.)	78.5 cm (31 in.)	80 cm (31½ in.)	81.5 cm (32 in.)	83 cm (32½ in.)	86 cm (33¾ in.)	87.5 cm (34½ in.)

*Choose your size based on the hip measurements, as the waist can be made smaller or bigger by changing the length of the elastic. The length is measured from the top of the waistband to the finished hem. The crotch length is measured from the top of the waistband front to back.

TEE

	XS/S	S/M	M/L	L/XL	XL/2XL	2XL/3XL	3XL/4XL	4XL/5XL	5XL/6XL
CHEST/HIP	90.5 cm (35½ in.)	98 cm (38½ in.)	105.5 cm (41½ in.)	113 cm (44½ in.)	120.5 cm (47½ in.)	128 cm (50½ in.)	135.5 cm (53½ in.)	143 cm (56¼ in.)	150.5 cm (59¼ in.)
BODY LENGTH*	68.5 cm (27 in.)	70 cm (27½ in.)	71.5 cm (28 in.)	73 cm (28¾ in.)	74.5 cm (29¼ in.)	76 cm (30 in.)	77.5 cm (30½ in.)	79 cm (31 in.)	80.5 cm (31½ in.)
SLEEVE LENGTH*	41.5 cm (16⅜ in.)	43 cm (17 in.)	44.5 cm (17½ in.)	46 cm (18 in.)	47.5 cm (18¾ in.)	49 cm (19¼ in.)	50.5 cm (19¾ in.)	52 cm (20½ in.)	53.5 cm (21 in.)

*The body length is measured from shoulder to finished hem. The sleeve length is measured from neck to finished hem, as the sleeve has a dropped shoulder.

TRACING AND CUTTING OUT YOUR PATTERNS

The PDF pattern downloads come with options for both A0 printing and A4/US letter paper. When printing the A4/US letter paper, set the scale to 100%, measure the text square and follow the taping guide to see which order to stick your pages together in.

UNDERSTANDING PATTERN SYMBOLS

1. **Size guidelines:** Each size is marked on the pattern piece with a different thickness of line.
2. **Grainline:** This indicates the direction in which you should lay your pattern piece on the fabric. Some pattern pieces have a grainline going in both directions; this means you can lay this pattern piece on the fabric either widthways or lengthways, depending on what works best for your layout plan.
3. **Alternative pattern shapes and details:** The dashed line indicates an alternative pattern option (for example, the shorts cutting line on the Comfort Pants front and back legs).
4. **Notch:** This is a small cut that you should make at this point on your fabric when cutting out. It indicates hem turn-ups and where certain pattern pieces fit together. Do not cut your notches more than 5 mm (¼ in.) deep.
5. **Pleats:** The dotted line and arrow indicate in which direction to fold a pleat. Join the pleat together, notch to notch, in the direction shown by the arrow.
6. **Dot:** These dots indicate where your welt pockets should be placed for each size. Mark them on your garment with a dissolvable fabric marker pen or a sharp piece of chalk.

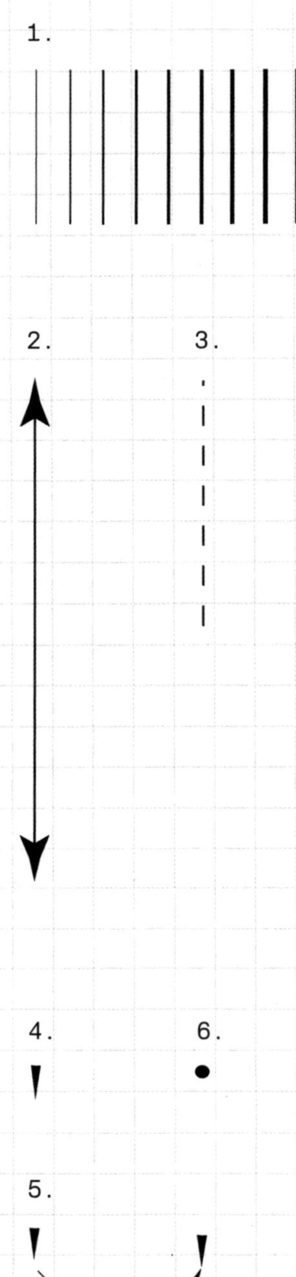

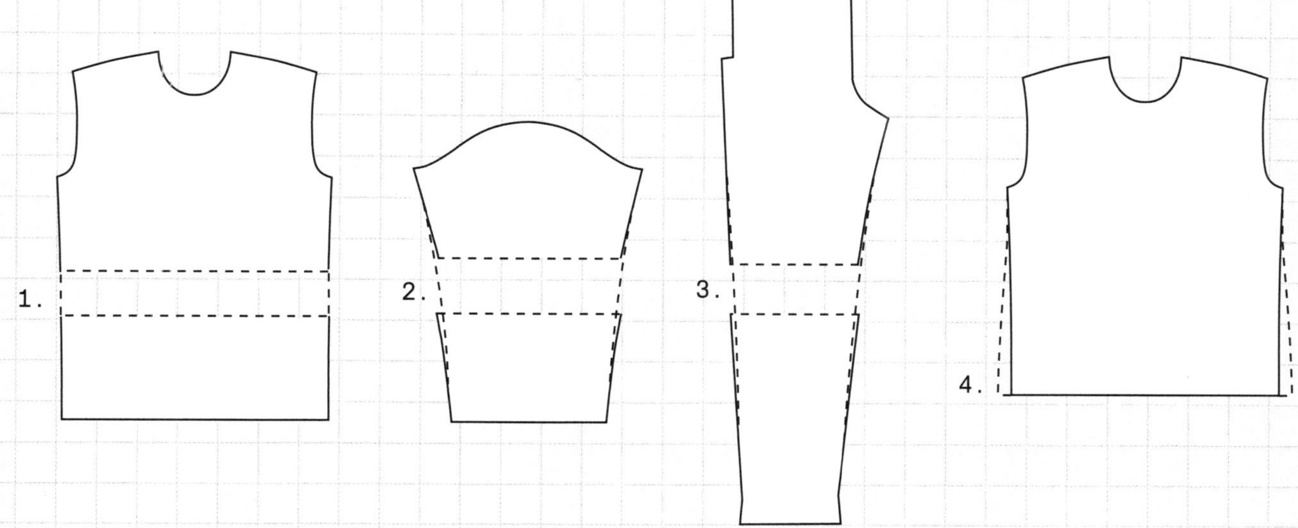

PATTERN ADJUSTMENTS

Being unisex shapes, these patterns have a relaxed fit and quite straight sides (i.e. not a lot of shaping). You can make simple adjustments to your patterns by, for example, adding a little more room at the hips or shaping in slightly at the waist. You can also change the lengths of all the pieces according to your preference. If you plan to make pattern changes, we recommend that you first make a toile/sample garment and fit it to yourself and then apply your adjustments to the pattern.

For some general help on pattern adjustments and how to achieve them, see the diagrams above.

1/2/3: ADJUSTING LENGTHS

Check lengths on the size charts to see if you want to add or remove length from pattern pieces. Cut apart your pattern pieces at around the mid length point and lower or raise as required. Straight seams are pretty straightforward, as shown in diagram 1. Some pattern pieces have curved seams so for these you will need to smooth out the new lines as shown in diagrams 2 and 3. When adding length to a body or trouser/pant leg, make sure you add the same amount to the front and back pattern pieces.

4: ADDING SIDE-SEAM SHAPING TO A BODY

If you want to add shaping to accommodate, for example, a bit more room around the hips, add the shaping to the sides, creating a smooth line that gradually connects to the original side seams. Add the same amount of shaping to the front and back body pieces by tracing the new side-seam shape evenly on both pattern pieces.

TOOLS &

Here you will find our tips for working with fabric scraps as well as information on the most relevant tools and notions used throughout the book, to help you complete each project with ease. You will also find a list of the most commonly used sewing techniques for the three patterns we've provided, with colour images and step-by-step instructions.

TECHNIQUES

CHOOSING FABRICS AND WORKING WITH SCRAPS

All of the pieces in this book are made using fabric scraps that we have saved from our clothing production – anything from small, scrappy pieces to larger offcuts. We have predominantly used cotton and linen offcuts and have tried to keep similar fabric weights and structures together. Here are some of the things we recommend you do to keep your scraps organized, along with some suggestions on how choose which fabrics to use for new projects:

ORGANIZE YOUR SCRAPS

We organize all of our scraps by size and also by colours. We store our larger scraps (any pieces that are about 10 x 10 cm/4 x 4 in. or larger) in large wooden boxes, each labelled to have different fabrics in them – one box for checks/stripes/prints, one for block colours, one for light/cream/white, one for dark/navy/black and so on. For smaller scraps we do one of two things. We sew long, thin strips, around 2.5 cm (1 in.) wide (for example, cut-away selvedges and thinner offcuts from cutting out garments) into yarn balls to save for projects later on. We throw all other tiny scraps that don't work for yarn balls into a bag and use them either for stuffing (for example, for cushions) or as a surface texture (such as our Terrazzo Clutch on page 182).

USE SIMILAR FABRIC WEIGHTS AND TYPES

When choosing scraps for a new project, try to pick similar weights and fabric types, and also preferably light- to medium-weight fabrics when doing any sort of textile surface decoration, as the thicker your fabrics are the more bulk they can add to your project.

KEEP LIGHT AND DARK COLOURS APART

This is because the colours can bleed into each other when they are washed. Try not to put a dark navy denim with a light cream-coloured fabric, for example.

WASH FABRICS BEFORE USE

We recommend that you wash any larger offcuts or fabric off the roll before use. You can also patchwork together a bunch of larger unwashed fabrics to make your base fabric and then wash after this. If you are working in this way, try to keep the grainlines of all the pieces going in the same direction as shrinkage usually occurs most significantly along the length of the fabric, not the width.

TOOLS & NOTIONS

This is a list of the tools and notions you will find most useful to complete the projects in this book. Don't stress if you don't have everything in this list – you can improvise with some of these items, and we have suggested alternatives where appropriate. Many of these tools are general, while others, such as the gathering foot, are specific to certain projects. Refer to individual projects to see which of these tools and notions are required.

TOOLS

- Sewing machine
- Overlocker – if you don't have an overlocker, you can finish the seams with zig-zag stitch, or another type of seam finish such as binding
- Iron
- Embroidery hoop for appliqué – you can do without an embroidery hoop by doing some extra tacking by hand before sewing
- Tape measure
- Long ruler/right-angled ruler for marking quilting lines; if you don't have a long ruler, try making one from a piece of heavy card
- Scissors: long dressmaking shears for cutting fabric and small scissors for trimming threads
- Paper scissors for cutting out traced patterns – it's best not to use your fabric scissors to cut paper, as this will blunt them more quickly
- Card (ideally the thickness of a cereal box) for making sewing guides
- Sharp tailor's chalk or dissolvable fabric marker pen
- Hand sewing needles
- Seam ripper for cutting open buttonholes
- Pencil, tape and paper for tracing and sticking together pattern pieces (ideally large, thin sheets of paper)
- Pins
- Large safety pin to pull through elastic
- Loop turner to turn out rouleau loops
- Gathering foot for your sewing machine to gather in bias strips for decoration
- Masking tape

NOTIONS

- Threads (for sewing machine, overlocker and hand sewing)
- Elastic, 3 cm (1¼ in.) and 5 cm (2 in.) wide
- Bias binding, 4 cm (1½ in.) wide – purchase it ready made by the metre/yard or cut it yourself
- Buttons in various sizes
- Iron-on woven interfacing
- Wadding for quilting

ORGANIC COTTO
MADE

SEWING TECHNIQUES

These are some of the main sewing techniques used in the book. Here you can find beginner-friendly tips on sewing seams and attaching a patch pocket, as well as more advanced techniques specific to certain projects, such as making welt pockets and attaching a collar. All are great skills to add to your sewing repertoire.

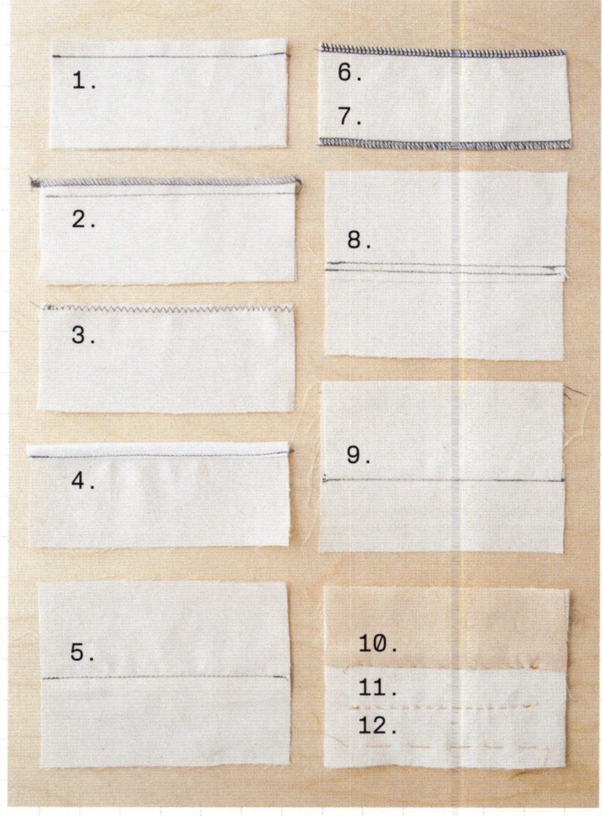

SEWING AND FINISHING SEAMS

All the seam allowances in this book are 1 cm (⅜ in.), unless otherwise specified. Most of the seams are sewn with straight stitch and finished by overlocking the seam allowances together, but you can finish raw edges with zig-zag stitching if you don't have an overlocker.

1. Seam sewn with straight stitch and a 1-cm (⅜-in.) seam allowance
2. Seam sewn with straight stitch and the seam allowances overlocked together
3. Zig-zag stitching
4. Binding (see page 37)
5. Understitching – done to secure a facing so it doesn't roll over to the right side of the garment
6. Four-thread overlocking
7. Three-thread overlocking
8. Raw felled seam (see opposite)
9. Stitch in the ditch – stitching in a previous seam line; in this book, we use it to secure backing fabric when sewing a waistband
10. Hand running stitch to attach lining
11. Hand running stitch
12. Hand basting stitch

Note: Understitching is a simple technique has a big impact on the hang and look of your garments, so don't be tempted to skip it. Once you have attached a facing to your garment, open out the pieces and press the seam allowances onto the facing. From the right side of the facing, and using matching thread, stitch about 1–2 mm (1/16 in.) or less from the seam line, securing the seam allowances to the facing. Once the facing is pressed to the inside of the garment, this stitching will pull the outer fabric over to the inside by a small amount, ensuring that none of the facing shows on the right side.

RAW FELLED SEAM

This is a version of a felled seam where there is an exposed raw edge on the right side of the fabric with two rows of stitching. The raw edges fray and soften with wear and the wrong side/inside of the fabric is finished neatly, with no raw edges exposed. The seam allowances when sewing a raw felled seam are 1.5 cm (⅝ in.) in total; one edge takes a 5-mm (¼-in.) seam allowance and the other edge takes a 1-cm (⅜-in.) seam allowance.

1. Place the pieces wrong sides together, with the edge of the top layer 5 mm (¼ in.) below the that of the bottom layer. Sew together 1 cm (⅜ in.) from the edge of the bottom layer.

2. Press the larger seam allowance down to cover the smaller one.

3. Topstitch the seam allowance down through all layers, sewing 5 mm (¼ in.) away from the first stitch line.

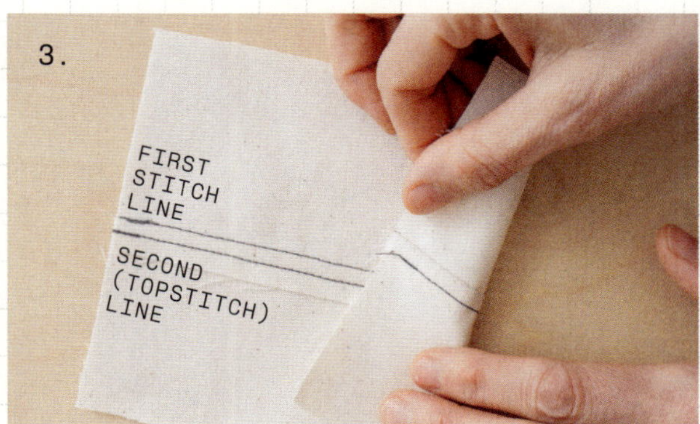

BUTTONS AND BUTTONHOLES

Refer to your sewing-machine manual for details of how to sew buttonholes. For buttonhole positioning, refer to the individual pattern or project information. The buttonholes can be sewn either vertically or horizontally. Vertical buttonholes are more suited to shirts and horizontal buttonholes look nice on coats and jackets.

1. Your buttonholes should always be the same size as the button you are using.

2. To cut open buttonholes, we recommend using a seam ripper – but take care as these can be very sharp! Start by inserting the pointy end of the seam ripper into the start of the buttonhole, then gently cut open slightly and poke the point out at the other end of the buttonhole before cutting completely open. This will ensure that you don't accidentally slice your buttonhole open more than needed.

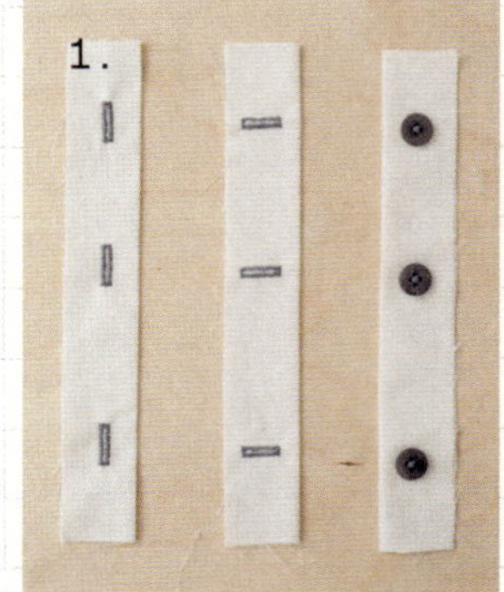

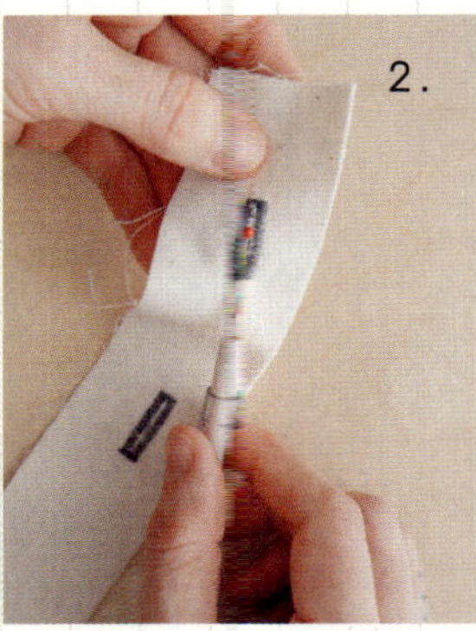

ROULEAU TIES

1. Fold the rouleau tie (a bias strip 2.5 cm/1 in. wide) in half, right sides together, and lightly finger press it.

2. Sew along the centre of the tie. Insert a loop turner at one end and push it all the way through the tube of fabric.

3. Hook a little of the fabric onto the loop turner, then pull to turn the tie right side out.

4. When the tie has been pulled right side out, the stitching will be hidden on the inside.

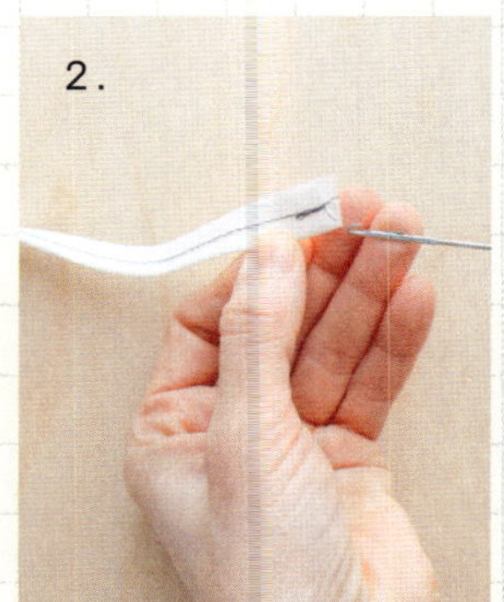

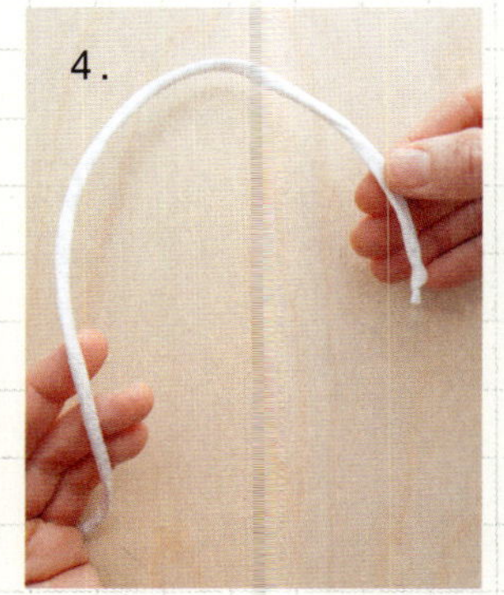

MACHINE QUILTING

1. Place a piece of wadding against the wrong side of your outer fabric. Baste the outer fabric and wadding together with some long diagonal running stitches in a contrasting thread colour (this makes it easier to see the basting stitches when you want to pull them out later).

2. Draw your quilting lines with a ruler and a dissolvable fabric marker pen. Here we have drawn diagonal lines 10 cm (4 in.) apart. Do this in both directions so that you end up with a grid of diamond-shaped quilting lines.

3. Roll your fabric up from one corner (the direction you roll should be in line with the stitch lines you will now sew). Rolling your fabric becomes more important the larger the piece you are working with is, as it helps to keep the fabric neat and out of the way while you are sewing the quilting lines. Stitch in your quilting lines with a straight stitch through all layers, unrolling the fabric a little at a time as needed.

4. Now repeat step 3 with the stitch lines going in the other direction.

5. Once you've sewn all the quilting lines, pull out your basting stitches and steam the piece with an iron to remove the drawn lines.

1.

2.

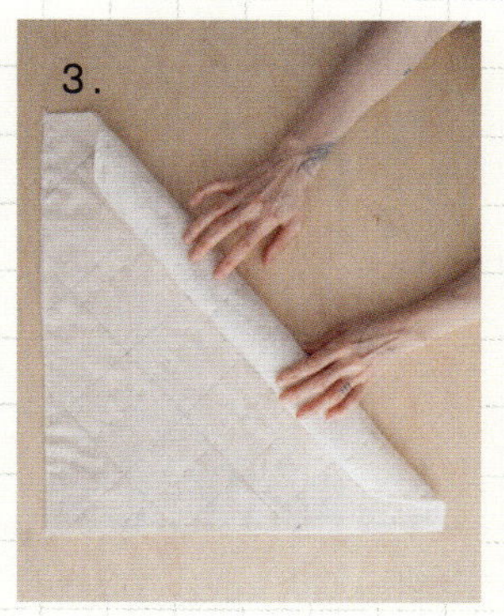
3.

4.

5.

WELT POCKET: 3 STYLES

Here we will take you through three different welt pockets: a side-seam welt pocket (used in our Comfort Pants), a back welt pocket (also on the Comfort Pants) and an angled welt pocket, used in our Quilted Coat – it is similar to the back welt pocket, but done on an angle.

SIDE-SEAM WELT POCKET

1. Fold the welt in half lengthways, wrong sides together, and stitch along all the raw edges, about 8 mm (¼ in.) away from the edges. Place the raw edge of the welt on the right side of the pocket facing along the cut-out section and sew in place, using a 1-cm (⅜-in.) seam allowance and finishing 1 cm (⅜ in.) past the cut-out corner of the facing.

2. Place the pocket facing with the welt attached along the cut-out section of the front leg side seam, right sides together. Topstitch the facing to the pants, following the exact same stitch line from the last step.

3. Cut into the corners of both the pocket facing layer and the front leg layer (do not cut the actual welt part), getting as close to the corner as you can.

4. Turn the pocket facing to the wrong side and press in place, turning under the corners of the pocket facing and front leg so you can see how the welt pocket should look when finished. Now carefully open out the front leg and facing so that you can pin the cut-out sections of the side seam in place against the short end of the welt.

5. Before you sew, check your pinning from the outside to make sure that the welt is sitting neatly.

6. Now stitch these sections to the short end of the welt, getting as close to the cut-out points as you can.

7. Topstitch through all layers close to the seam line of the welt along the long side and the bottom short end.

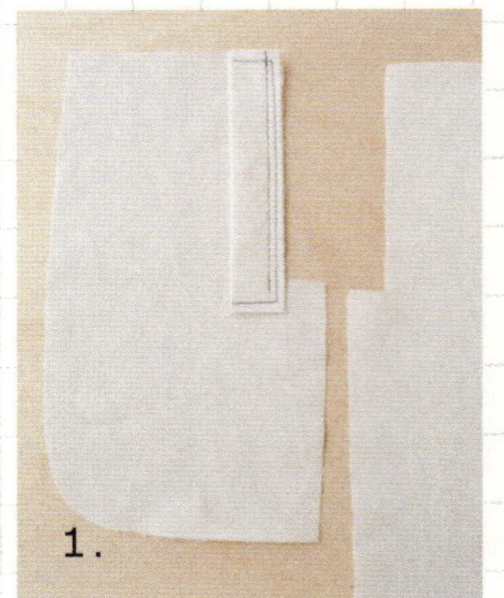
1.

2.

3.

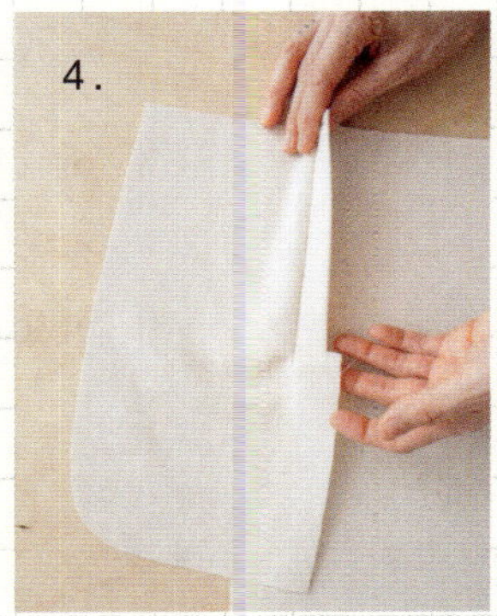
4.

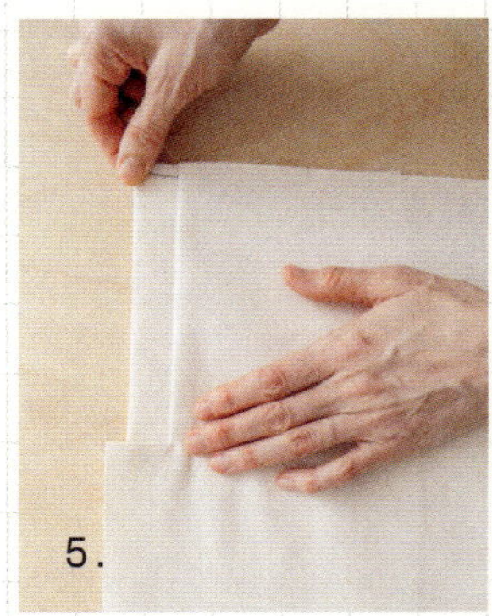
5.

6.

7.

8. Place the pocket lining against the pocket facing, right sides together, lining up the top edges and curves (photo 8a). Pin and sew the two pieces together around the curved edge, then overlock the seam allowances together (photo 8b). Take great care not to stitch through the leg piece!

9. Sew the lower part of the pocket bag to the side seam of the pants, sewing right up to the start of the welt.

10. Place the front and back legs right sides together along the side seam (photo 10a). Sew in place, following the exact same stitch line as you get to the lower part of the welt/pocket bag; this will ensure that you sew far enough in for the welt to sit neatly against the back side seam. (Take care not to sew through the welt.) Overlock the seam allowances together, then press them towards the back. From the right side, the pocket should look as shown in photo 10b.

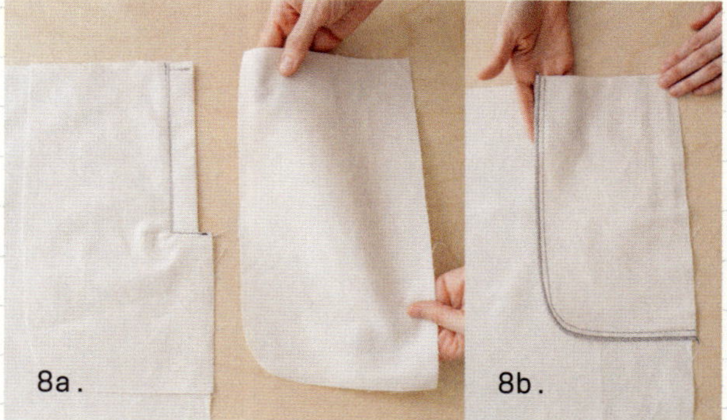
8a. 8b.

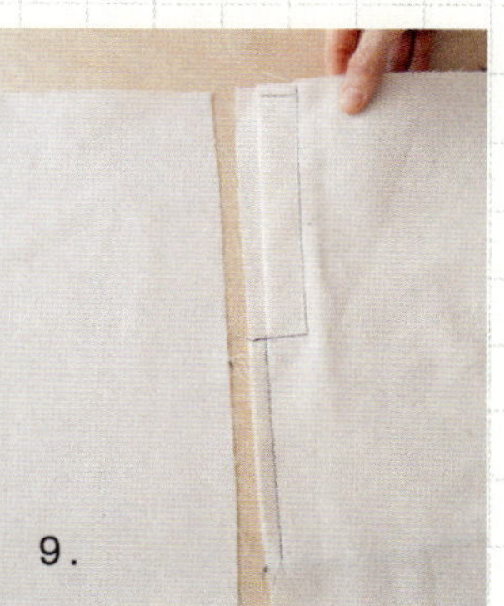
9.

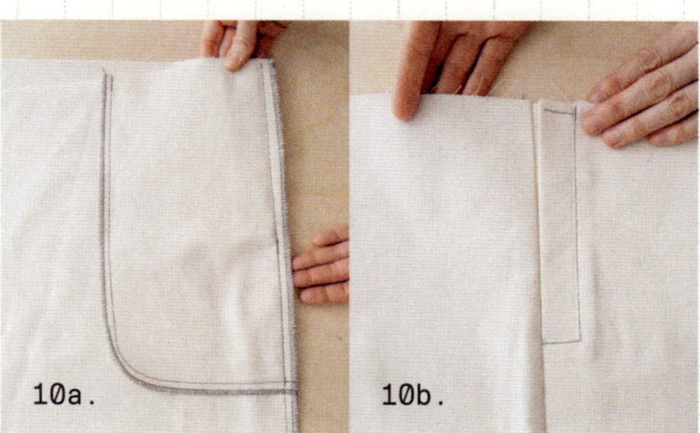
10a. 10b.

BACK WELT POCKET

1. Attach a rectangle of iron-on interfacing to the wrong side of the pants, roughly in the centre of where the welt will sit. This will add strength to the fabric. The interfacing piece should be approximately 5 x 18 cm (2 x 7 in.).

2. Fold the welt in half lengthways, wrong sides together, and stitch along all the raw edges, about 8 mm (¼ in.) away from the edges. Place the long raw edge of the welt along the top edge of the pocket facing, right sides together, and sew in place, starting and finishing about 1.5 cm (⅝ in.) away from each end.

3. With right sides together, place the pocket facing with the welt attached against the back leg, lining it up with the placement dots for the welt pocket, and pin in place. The top edge of the pocket/welt should be placed just below the dots and centred between them. Topstitch the welt/pocket facing to the pants exactly along the previous stitch line, finishing about 1.5 cm (⅝ in.) away from each end.

4. Turn the back leg over to the wrong side and draw a rectangle on the interfacing, with the previous stitch line as the bottom edge of the rectangle. The rectangle should measure the width of the stitching line and be 2.4 cm (just under 1 in.) high – or just 1 mm smaller than the height of the finished welt. Draw a line through the centre of the rectangle and a short diagonal line going from the centre line into each corner, as shown.

5. Cut along the centre line and into the points, as shown here, getting as close to the points as you can. Make sure you don't cut the welt when you do this.

6. Turn the pocket facing through the slit to the wrong side and press in place along all four edges, turning under 1 cm (⅜ in.) all the way around. Once you've pressed it in place, you'll be able to see how the welt will look when finished.

1.

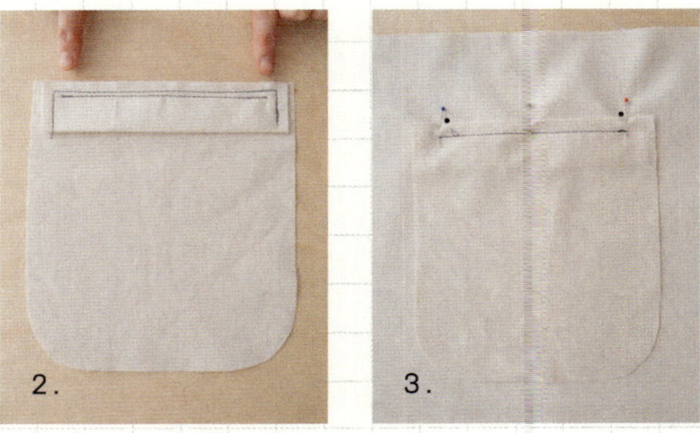
2. 3.

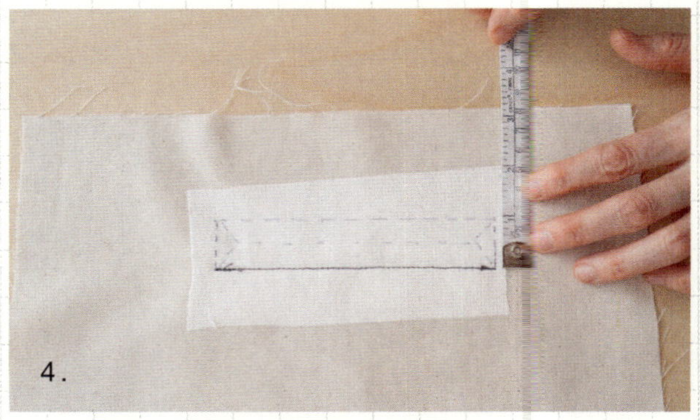
4.

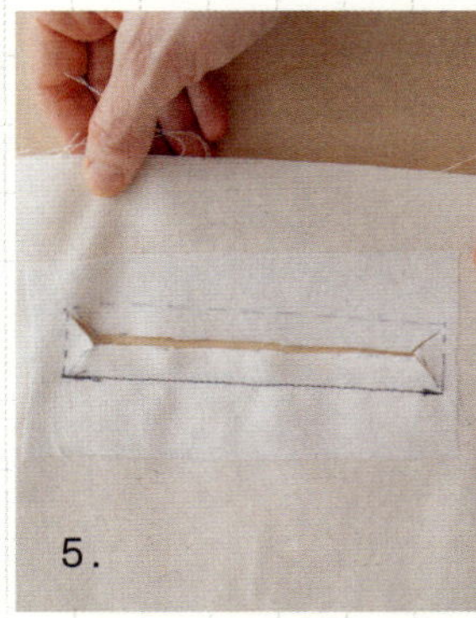
5.

6.

7. Fold back each end of the cut-out section so that you can pin each triangular flap in place against the short end of the welt. Before you sew, check your pinning from the right side to make sure that the welt is sitting neatly. Now stitch these sections to the short end of the welt, getting as close to the cut-out corners as you can.

8. Topstitch through all layers along the two short ends and the long bottom edge, close to the seam line of the welt.

9. Turn the pant leg over to the wrong side. Place the pocket lining against the pocket facing, right sides together, lining up the curves and the top of the pants. (Sometimes the top edge can be a little out of alignment, so you can simply trim away the excess along the top of the pocket lining to match the pants and facing placement.)

10. Carefully fold down the top part of the pants (photo 10a) and pin in place to sew the top section of the cut-out rectangle to the pocket lining. Stitch down neatly, going as close to the corneers on the rectangle of the welt as you can (photo 10b).

11. Press in place from the right side and topstitch close to the welt seam, to finish the rectangular stitch line around the welt.

12. Finally, sew together the pocket facing and pocket lining and then either bind the edge (as shown here) or overlock the seam allowances together.

7.

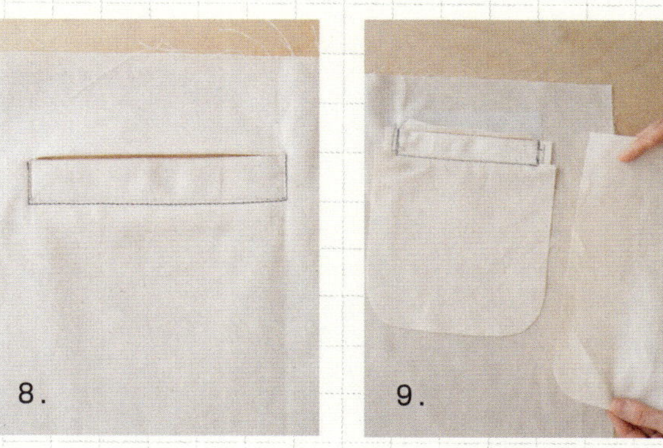
8.

9.

10a.

10b.

11.

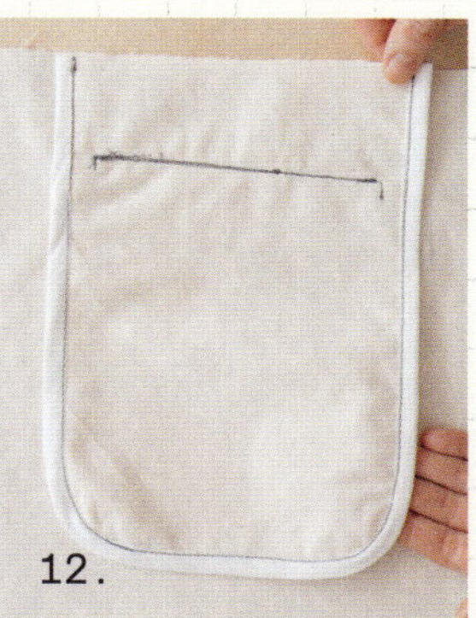
12.

Tip: To make sure your welt fits perfectly into your cut-out rectangle, we recommend checking the size of your finished welt height after attaching it in step 3 by measuring it to the millimetre. The finished height of your rectangle should always be 1 mm smaller than the finished height of your welt. This will ensure that the rectangle is not cut too big or small, making a perfect fit for your welt.

ANGLED WELT (COAT) POCKET

1. Fold the welt in half lengthways, wrong sides together, and stitch along all the raw edges, about 8 mm (¼ in.) away from the edges. Overlock the bottom (slightly longer) edge of the pocket facing. With the wrong side of the facing against the right side of the underlining, sew the pocket facing to the top of the pocket underlining around all edges about 8 mm (¼ in.) away from the edges.

2. Place the raw long edge of the welt on the top edge of the pocket top lining, right sides together, and sew in place, starting about 1.5 cm (⅝ in.) away from the straight end of the welt and stitching for 15 cm (6 in.).

3. Place the pocket top lining with the welt attached on the coat, right sides together, lining it up with the placement dots for the welt pocket. Pin in place. The top edge of the pocket/welt should be placed just below the dots and the first dot (the one that sits slightly higher on the body) should sit approximately 2 cm (¾ in.) in from the outer edge of the pocket, on the side that curves down. Topstitch the pocket top lining/welt to the coat exactly along the previous stitch line.

4. Now follow steps 4–12 of the Back Welt Pocket, using the stitch line on the wrong side to mark a rectangle up from that point. The height of the rectangle should be 2.9 cm/1³⁄₁₆ in. (1 mm smaller than the finished welt size of 3 cm/1¼ in. for the coat). Cut open the rectangle through the centre and cut triangles into the points. When you get to the stage of placing the pocket lining on the pocket facing, line up the top edges of the pieces and the curves and notches of the pocket bag should match (photo 4a). Stitch together and overlock the seams together (photo 4b).

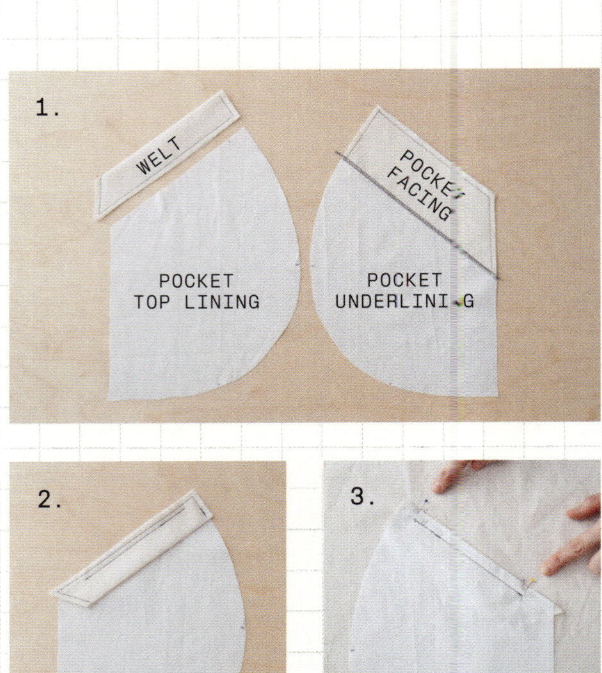

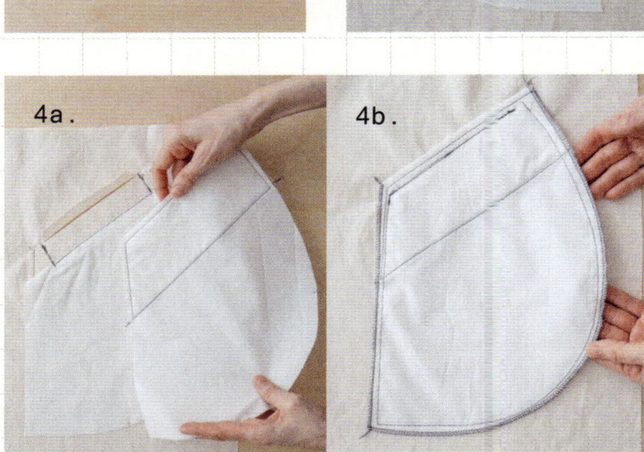

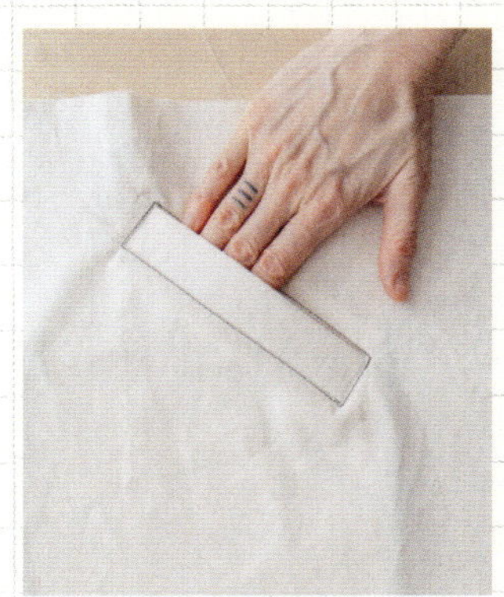

PATCH POCKET

1. Press the top straight edge of the patch pocket to the wrong side by 1 cm (⅜ in.), then press it down to the wrong side a second time to the notches. Topstitch the turn-down in place close to the fold line. Work a second row of stitching about 8 mm (¼ in.) away from the first one. Stitch around the raw edges of the sides/bottom about 8 mm (¼ in.) from the edge, using a long stitch to ease in the curves slightly. Press in the sides/bottom to the wrong side by about 1 cm (⅜ in.).

2. Place the wrong side of the pocket on the right side of the garment. Pin in place and topstitch around the side and bottom edges close to the fold line, working a diagonal stitch line at both top corners to strengthen the pocket.

BINDING

This shows how to attach binding to the sleeve split of the Workwear Jacket, but the same method can be used to attach binding to any straight edge. Use a pre-cut binding 4 cm (1½ in.) wide.

1. Place the right side of the binding on the wrong side of the fabric and sew in place with an 8-mm (¼-in.) seam allowance (photo 1a). If you are sewing the binding onto the sleeve split, you will need to angle the fabric out when you get to the top point of the split, as shown in photo 1b, before sewing the other side.

2. Press the binding down, away from the sleeve.

3. Fold the unsewn edge of the binding up by approximately 1 cm (⅜ in.) and press.

4. Then turn the binding over to the right side of the fabric, so that the fold covers the first stitch line.

5. Press, pin in place and stitch the binding down, close to the fold line.

1. PATCH POCKET
2.
1a. BINDING
1b.
2.
3.
4.
5.

ATTACHING A SLEEVE CUFF

1. Attach the sleeve split binding (see page 37).
2. From the wrong side of the sleeve, sew a diagonal line of stitching along the top edge of the binding to hold it neatly in place at the top of the split.
3. Sew the pleat down between the notches and then turn the binding to the wrong side on the side of the split that's closest to the pleat. Topstitch the pleat in place, keeping your stitches just within the seam allowance.
4. Fold the sleeve cuffs in half, right sides together, and sew the side edges. Turn the cuffs right side out and press.
5. Line up the raw edges of the cuff and sleeve (photo 5a), with the cuff against the wrong side of the sleeve, and stitch, stitching through only one layer of the cuff (photo 5b). The cuff should fit the sleeve hem perfectly.
6. Pull the cuff down and turn the sleeve right side up. Press. Turn under the raw edge of the cuff by 1 cm (3/8 in.). Pin in place over the sleeve hem, covering the first stitch line.
7. Topstitch the cuff across the top through all layers, close to the fold line. Then topstitch around the sides and edges of the cuff, about 8 mm (1/4 in) away from the edges.

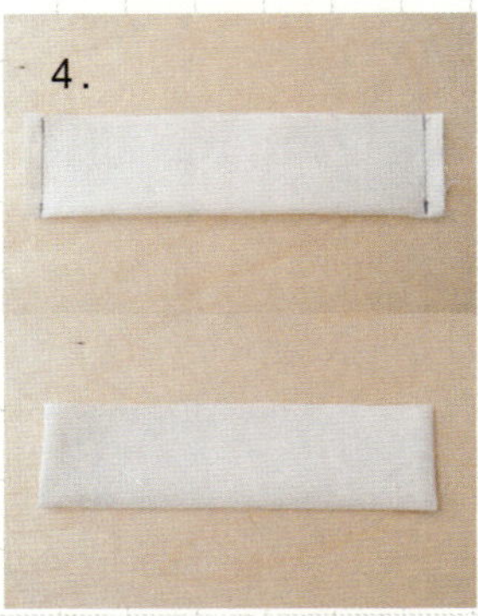

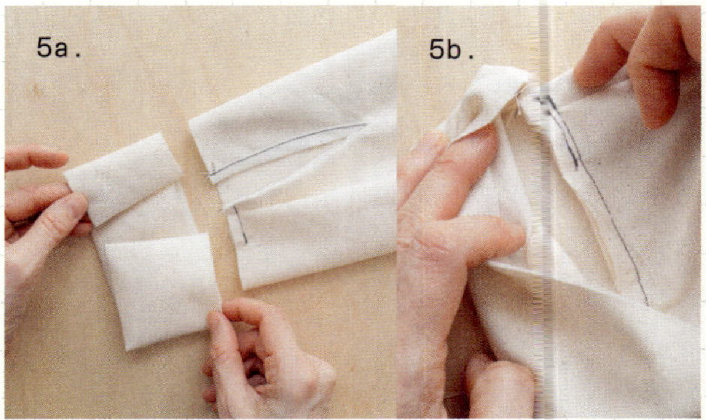

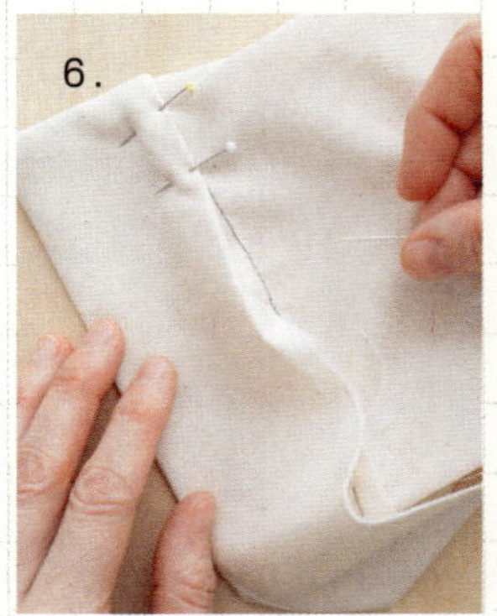

ATTACHING A COLLAR AND FACINGS

1. Place the two collar pieces right sides together and sew along the bottom curved edge with a 1-cm (⅜-in.) seam allowance (photo 1a). Press the seam allowances down. Open out the collar and understitch (see page 28) on the right side of the undercollar (the piece that is destined to be on the underside) close to the stitch line, to hold the seam allowances in place (photo 1b).

2. Fold the collar pieces right sides together, with the seam line at the bottom. Sew along the short ends, then turn the collar right side out and press.

3. Topstitch all around the collar, 8 mm (¼ in.) from the edge. The underside of the collar may be slightly higher than the top because of the understitching, but this will ensure that the underside will not roll out when it is attached to the jacket.

4. Attach the collar to the neckline, with the underside of the collar against the right side of the neck. The collar should start and end at the notch nearest the centre front edge on the neckline of each front piece, and the shoulders and centre back of the neck should match the other notches on the collar.

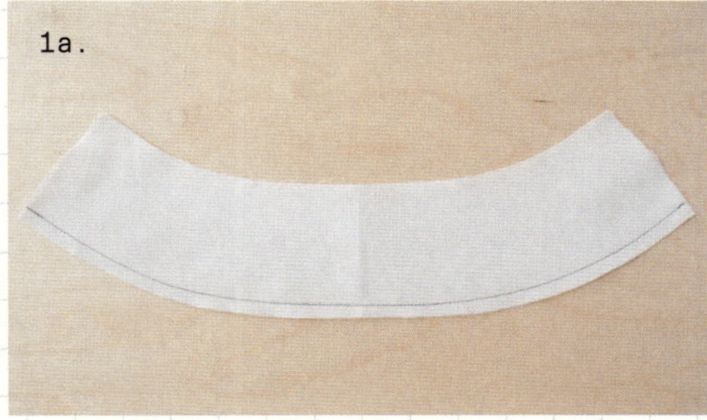

1a.

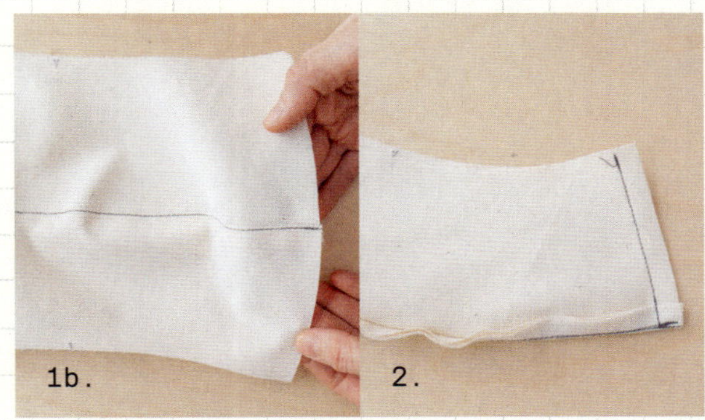

1b. 2.

3.

4.

5. With right sides together, sew the front and back facing pieces together at the shoulder seams and press the seams open. Bind the outer raw edges of the facings (the opposite side to the neckline) all the way around (photo 5a). With right sides together, pin the facing around the neck of the body, matching the shoulder seams and sandwiching the collar in between. Sew all the way around (photo 5b).

6. Press the seam allowances down, towards the body of the garment. Between the shoulders, understitch the back facing.

7. With right sides together, pin the front facings to the jacket fronts and sew from the neck point down to the hem (photo 7a), turning down the seam allowances neatly at the top neck point (photo 7b). Sew together with a 1-cm (⅜-in.) seam allowance.

8. Turn the facings to the right side and press the facings and seam allowances away from the body all the way down both centre fronts.

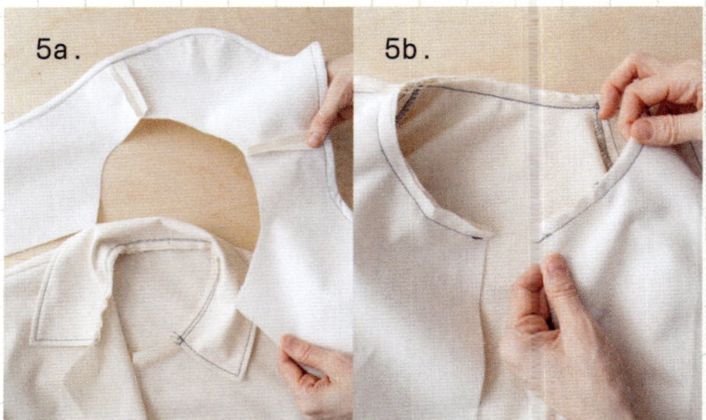

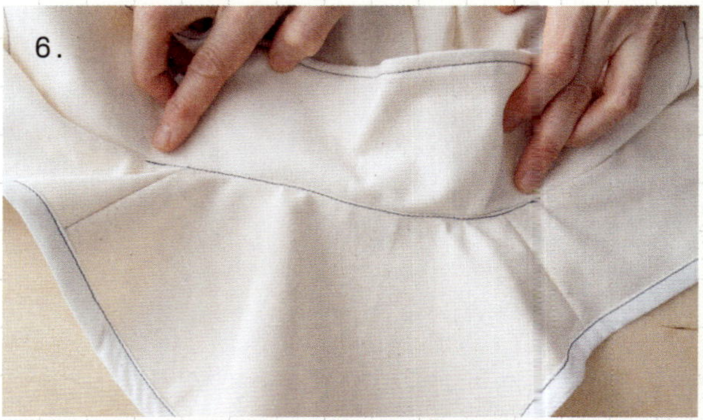

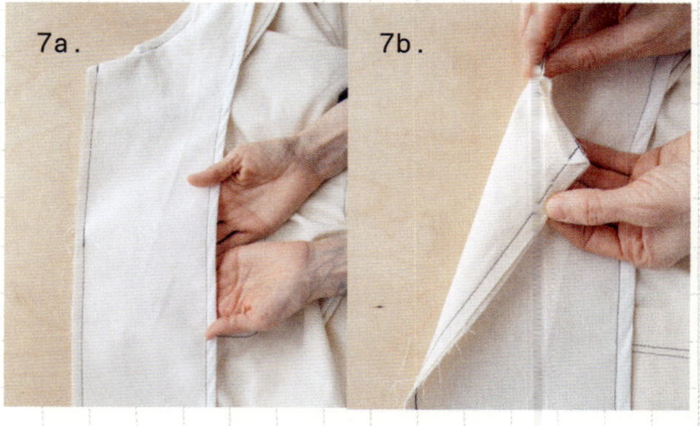

9. With right sides together, fold the facings back onto the garment front along the cut-out section. Sew along the bottom edge.

10. Turn the facings right side out and press neatly in place. Press the rest of the hem of the jacket to the wrong side by 1 cm (⅜ in.), then press up a second time to the finished hem line (lining up with the centre front and side notches). Pin the hem in place all the way around. Alternatively, you can bind this section of the hem and then press it up as far as the finished hem line.

11. Fold the collar up, away from the garment, so that you don't catch it in the stitching (photo 11a). Starting at the front neckline, topstitch all around through all layers on the front neckline, centre front edges and the section of the centre front hems that have a facing, stitching 8 mm (¼ in.) from the edges (photo 11a). Once you reach the end of the facing, turn and work a short vertical line of stitching, then turn again and continue stitching around the rest of the hem, close to the fold line (photo 11b) and on round in one continuous line until you get back to your start point.

12. Finally, press the back facing in place on the back body, wrong sides together. Pin in place between the back shoulders and topstitch through all layers, following the curved line of the bottom of the facing.

9.

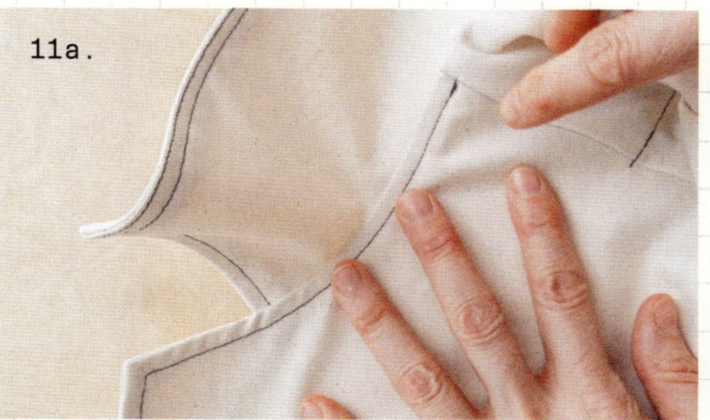
11a.

11b.

12.

BINDING A WAISTBAND

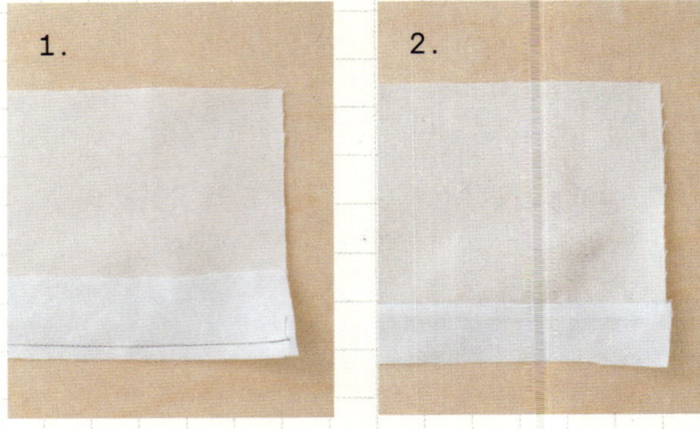

1. With right sides together, sew one edge of the binding to one long raw edge of the waistband, with an 8-mm (¼-in.) seam allowance.
2. Press the binding down.
3. Fold the excess binding to the wrong side. Sew the binding down close to the fold line of the binding, on the right side of the waistband piece, through all layers. The underside of the waistband will still have the raw edge of the binding exposed. This will be covered once the waistband is fully attached to your pants or skirt. We do it this way to reduce bulk.

ATTACHING A WAISTBAND AND INSERTING ELASTIC

1. Bind one long edge of the waistband, as described above. With right sides together, sew the short edges of the waistband together. Press the seam open.
2. With the garment wrong side out and the waistband right side out, place the waistband inside the garment, lining up the centre back seams and centre front points (photo 2a). Sew the raw edge of the waistband to the garment (photo 2b).

3. Press the seam allowances and waistband up, then fold the waistband in half widthways, wrong sides together. The bound edge of the waistband should extend past the seam between the garment and waistband by approximately 1 cm (⅜ in.) – photo 3a. Press and pin in place. From the front of the garment, stitch in the ditch just below the seam of the waistband, securing the bound edge of the waistband as you go and leaving a 5-cm (2-in.) opening near the centre back (photo 3b).

4. Attach a large safety pin to one end of the elastic and insert it into the opening near the centre back (photo 4a). Pull the elastic through all the way around, then join the ends of the elastic at the centre back with two rows of stitching (photo 4b).

5. Close the opening near the centre back by stitching in the ditch.

6. Spread the elastic evenly through the waistband, then work a vertical line of stitching at the centre back, side seams (lining up with the end of the welts) and centre front to hold the elastic in place and stop it from twisting.

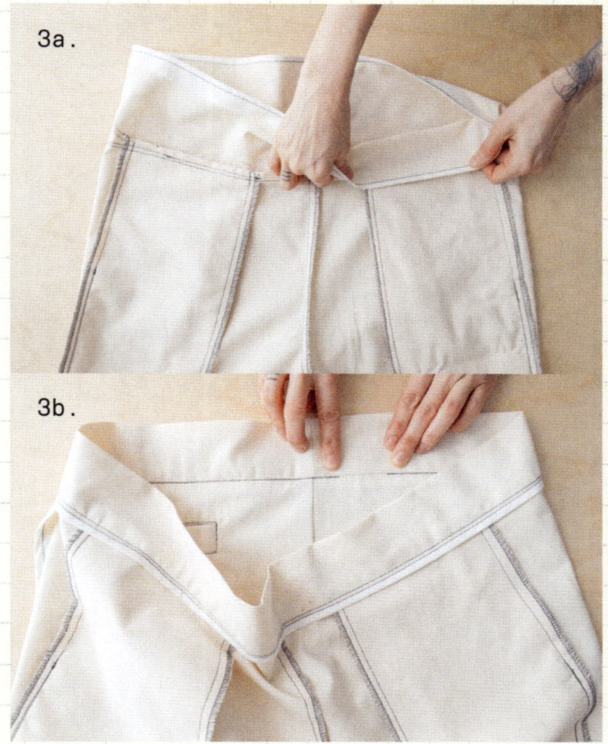

3a.

3b.

4a.

4b.

6.

Tip: When sewing down the waistband in step 3 (stitching in the ditch), it is easiest if the pants are turned inside out, as shown in the photo. This means that the excess fabric is out of the way and it is easier to sew neatly.

METHOD:

PATCHWORK

Patchwork was the first method we ever worked with to use up scraps and it is probably the most well-known method, which is why we want to start here. It is super versatile and a great way of using up leftover fabrics to make wearable and unique garments. You can patchwork crazy colours and patterns together to make a statement piece or keep it neutral and work with tone on tone and similar textures to make a piece that can be worn with most things in your wardrobe.

In this method we will take you step by step through the process of putting together patchwork fabrics and planning out your pieces. We mostly use only squares and rectangles, and in all the projects that use this method in this book, the patches have straight edges only.

Once you have learnt the basics, you can refer to the seam finish variations on pages 52–53 for more ways of sewing to add detailing to your patchwork.

QUILTED COAT

WORKWEAR JACKET

SHORT SHORTS

RE-MAKE JACKET

COMFORT PANTS

PATCHWORK TEE

FABRICS

Before you choose your fabric scraps, think about the finished size of the project. For example, if you're making a large project, such as the Quilted Coat, it's generally best to use larger scraps for the patchwork. Not only will this have more visual impact, but it'll also be a lot quicker to sew. For a small-scale project such as a purse or a table mat, you can get away with using smaller fabric scraps.

The more you work with this method, the better you will get at knowing what size of scraps is suitable for what type of project.

If you start by choosing a bunch of scraps in colours and textures that you like together, then you are already on your way to planning the patchwork. This means that you don't need to think too hard about which fabrics go with which when planning the sizes and locations of the different patchwork pieces.

A VERY IMPORTANT NOTE ON COLOURS

Do not mix dark unwashed fabrics with light-coloured fabrics (for example, a raw denim scrap with a white cotton drill): the first time you wash the garment, the dark colours could very likely bleed. Instead, choose similar colours or work with fabric scraps that have already been thoroughly washed.

PLANNING

The way you plan and sew together your patchwork pieces will vary depending on the garment or project you are making. One way to work is to build up the amount of patchwork fabric you need using each individual pattern piece as a guide. This is ideal with certain patterns, as it is a little less wasteful.

At other times, it can be easier to build up an entire piece of fabric first, especially if the pattern you are using has a particularly efficient cutting layout.

We will show you how to plan and sew using a guide marked on your cutting surface in order to build up the pieces in the most clear and efficient way, but the process of building up patchwork using a pattern piece is essentially the same. You can use either of these approaches – just make sure that you clearly establish which is the straight grain of your fabric or pattern piece each time. Each patchwork project in this book will specify which option is easier to work with.

1. Work out the size of your patchwork by measuring the length and width required on your surface and placing a small piece of masking tape on each outer corner. For this example we are making a patchwork piece that will have a finished size of 40 x 40 cm (16 x 16 in.), but you can work with much bigger sizes than this using the same technique. Position your outer boundaries a few centimetres (an inch or so) larger than the finished piece you want to make, as your fabric can often shrink in a little after it has been sewn and pressed.

2. Straighten the edges of the scraps so that they are rectangular or square in shape. Place your first fabric scrap on one of the outer edges, making sure you keep the straight grain going along the horizontal or vertical edges of your boundary.

3. Place the next piece overlapping the first one along one of the straight edges (photo 3a). Your overlap should always be double the seam allowance you plan to use when sewing the pieces together later. For this example, we are working with a 1-cm (⅜-in.) seam allowance, which means that we need to overlap all the edges by 2 cm (¾ in.) when the fabrics are lying flat (photo 3b).

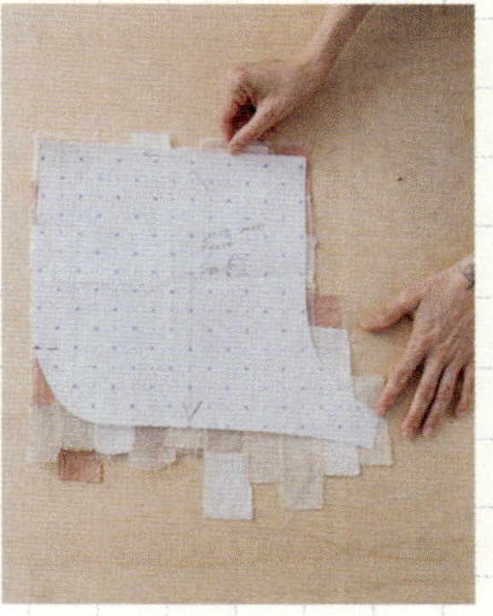

USING PATTERN PIECE AS A GUIDE

BUILDING UP AN ENTIRE PIECE OF FABRIC

1.

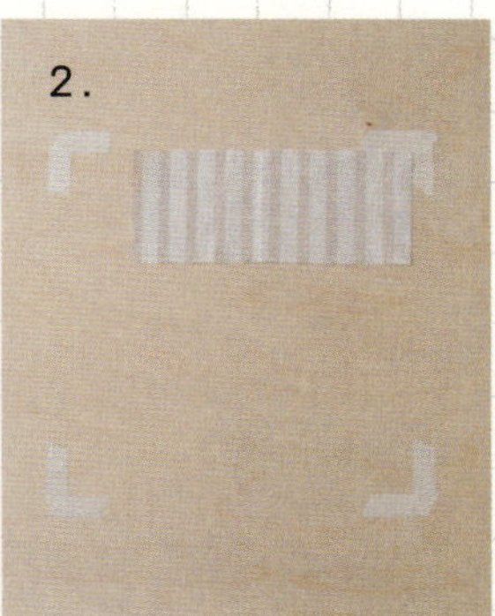

2.

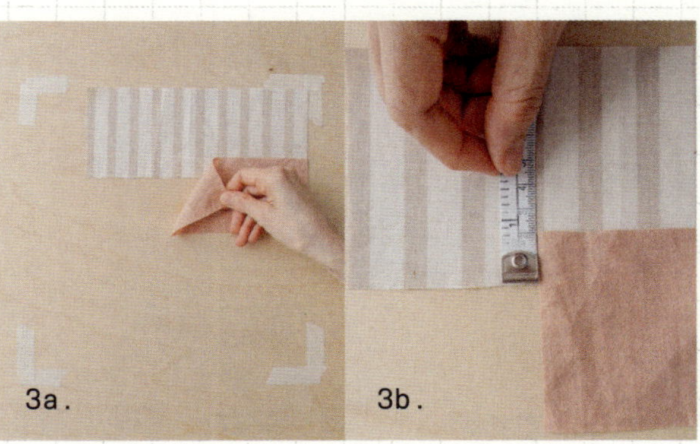

3a.

3b.

4. Continue adding patchwork pieces in this way, trimming the fabric scraps as you go.

5. Once you have covered the whole area, you can plan how you will sew your patchwork pieces together (photo 5a). To do this, start by organizing your pieces into smaller units. It will be a little different every time, but the key is to try to make it as simple and efficient as possible.

   In this example, we have separated several units: a vertical row of grey and white on the left, and four horizontal rows on the right (photo 5b).

6. Once you've organized your smaller units, you can begin to sew them together (photo 6a), working in the most logical way possible. Here we sewed together the four horizontal units (photo 6b) and then joined the long vertical unit to them (photo 6c). Now finish your seam allowances as desired (see below).

4.

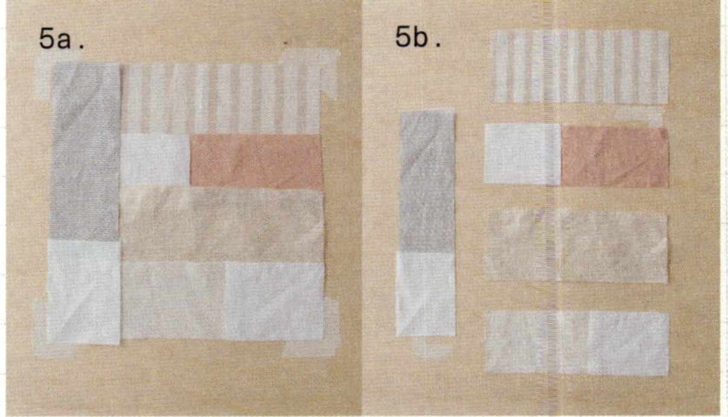
5a. 5b.

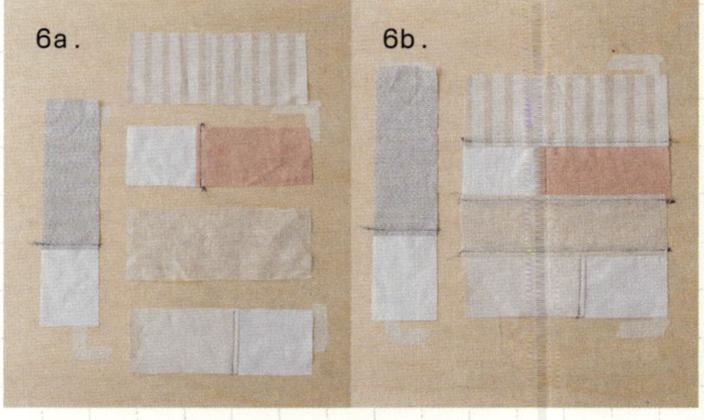
6a. 6b.

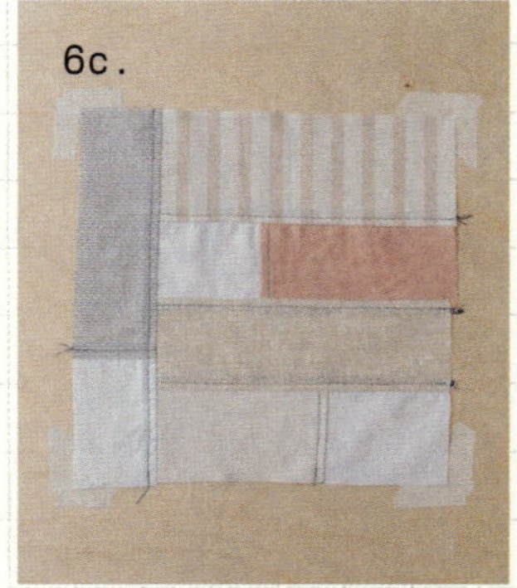
6c.

Note: In this example, we have sewn the pieces in each unit together with a straight stitch, using a 1-cm (⅜-in.) seam allowance, overlocked the seam allowances together, pressed the seam allowances to one side, and then topstitched the seam allowances down. There are more examples of seam finishes on pages 52–53.

TROUBLESHOOTING!

JOINING PATCHWORK SHAPES

Sometimes when organizing your pieces into units you may end up with what we call an 'L-shape situation', where you need to sew only a portion of a seam before you can attach another piece. Do not fear: just keep your steps structured and attach once piece at a time until all the pieces fit, as we have done here.

1. If we'd sewn the whole of the right-hand unit to the long denim rectangle at the top, it would have been tricky to attach the left-hand unit without getting messy joins and puckered seams.

2. By adding the dark green left-hand unit before completing the seam, we can then continue the horizontal seam neatly.

3. The pieces join up perfectly!

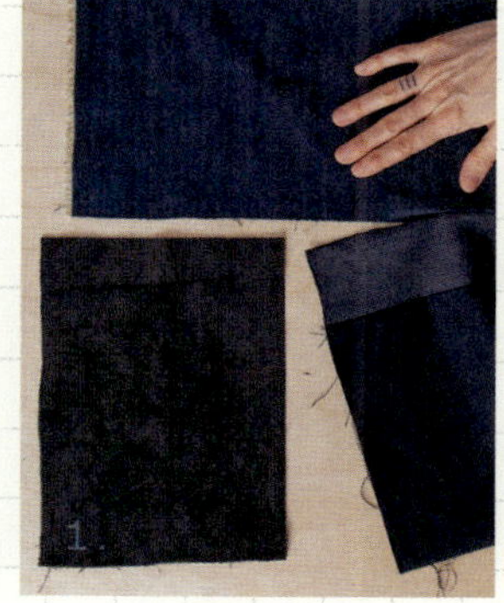
1.

2.

3.

JOINING LOTS OF SMALL PATCHWORK PIECES TOGETHER

Joining lots of small, even-sized pieces can be time consuming. The solution is to start a production line.

1. Plan out several long strips of small patchwork pieces that are all the same width. Sew the first two pieces of the first strip together and then, without cutting the threads, sew the first two pieces of the second strip together.

2. Continue joining consecutive pieces in the same way until you have the number of pieces you need in each strip, then cut the threads between them. This is known as chain piecing.

3. Repeat the chain-piecing process to zig-zag stitch over the seams on the right side (photos 3a and 3b), then cut apart the threads (photo 3c).

4. Finally sew all the long seams together, press the seams to one side, and zig-zag stich over the seam allowances, on the right side.

3a.

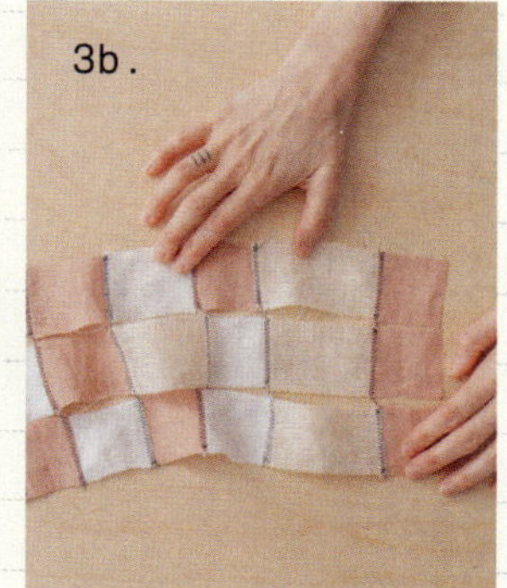
3b.

3c.

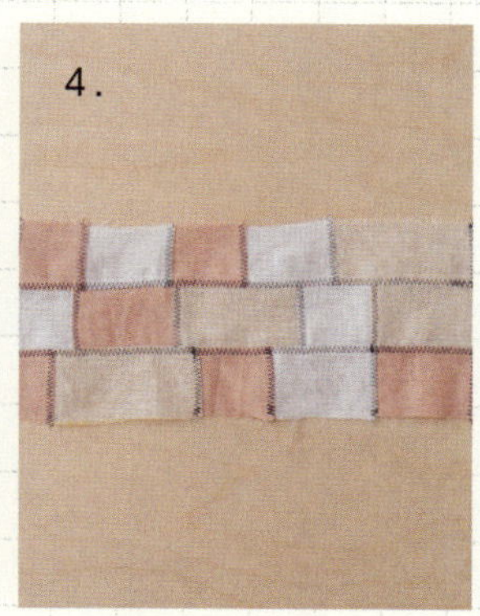
4.

SEAM FINISH VARIATIONS

This is the fun part! Here we will show you a bunch of other seam variations, all of which are used in the projects in this book. The seam finishes can make a big difference to the final outcome and can be a fun way to experiment with different ideas and textures – for example, leaving raw edges to fray or using topstitch (machine or by hand) to create more detailing.

1.

OPTIONS 1 AND 2: STITCH AND OVERLOCK

Sew the pieces together with straight stitch, overlock the seam allowances together, press the seams to one side and topstitch about 8 mm (¼ in.) from the seams. Option 1 shows the technique used with light-toned fabrics and option 2 with dark-toned fabrics.

2.

OPTION 3: RAW FELLED SEAMS

In this seam variation the patchwork pieces are sewn together a little like a felled seam: the seams on the wrong side of the fabric are finished neatly and the seams on the right side have a raw edge that frays in a really nice way with wash and wear. See page 29 for how to sew this seam.

3.

OPTION 4: EXPOSED SEAMS

For this sample we have used stretch fabrics and sewn them together with an overlocker, with the seams exposed on the right side of the fabric. Sew with the wrong sides of the fabric facing each other.

4.

OPTION 5: ZIG-ZAG TOPSTITCHING

The zig-zag stitching adds a nice detail on the outside. As an alternative to overlocking, it also helps to stop the fabric from fraying.

5.

OPTION 6: SEAMS PRESSED OPEN

This option is suitable for garments that you plan to line or quilted pieces that have a layer of wadding. Pressing the seams open, rather than to one side, makes for a nice, flat finish and reduces bulk.

6.

OPTION 7: QUILTING BY MACHINE

This is an extension of option 6. Place a layer of wadding underneath the patchwork fabric and quilt together with machine topstitching. You can use all sorts of stitch-line designs – vertical straight lines, horizontal straight lines, diagonal lines and so on. Here we have marked out diagonal lines in both directions to create a diamond-shaped grid. See page 31 for more on quilting.

7.

OPTION 8: QUILTING BY HAND

This is an extension of option 6. Place a layer of wadding underneath the patchwork fabric and quilt together with hand stitching. As with machine quilting, you can use all sorts of stitch-line designs – vertical straight lines, diagonal etc. Here we have hand stitched around each patchwork piece to outline the edges.

8.

COMFORT PANTS

The first pants we ever did for Helgrose were a tailored design with a fitted waistband and fly-front button closure. We loved them, but as we are all about ultra-wearability we set about creating a more comfortable variation. The result was an incredibly versatile pair of pants with an elasticated waist and a casual, relaxed fit that still retains a tailored feel with details like welt pockets and pleats. To this day, six years on from making that first pair, they are still an absolute favourite of ours and our customers! This version has been made with raw felled seams that will fray with washing, giving them a softer look. Hope you have fun with this make!

SKILL LEVEL ●●●●○

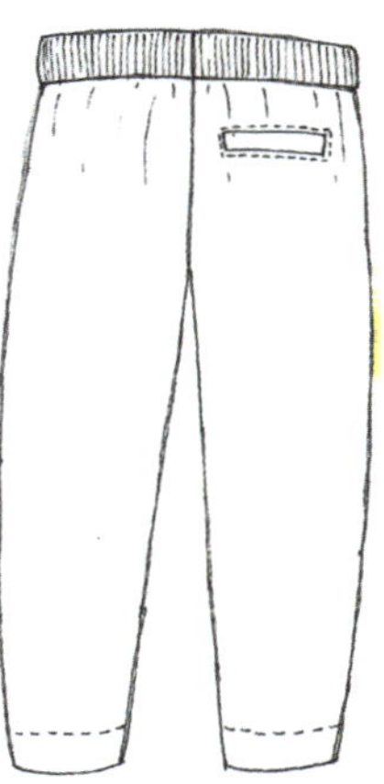

TECHNIQUES

Patchwork, raw felled seams

SIZES MADE

Size M worn by Ludjero and size M worn by Anna

FABRIC

Light- to medium-weight cotton off-cuts

Tip: The skill level of this project is relatively high because of the welt pockets. If you are not quite ready to tackle welts, you can add side-seam pockets to the fronts instead by cutting one pair of the pocket lining (F) pieces for each side, instead of using the pocket facing (E) with the welt, and you can add patch pockets to the back by using the hip pockets from the Workwear Jacket pattern. If you do this, make sure you follow the dashed Shorts line for the side-seam part of the front leg pattern, instead of cutting out the little rectangular section at the side.

NOTIONS

	XS	S	M	L	XL	2XL	3XL	4XL	5XL	6XL
ELASTIC: 5 CM (2 IN.) WIDE	70 cm (27½ in.)	75 cm (29½ in.)	80 cm (31½ in.)	85 cm (33½ in.)	90 cm (35½ in.)	95 cm (37½ in.)	100 cm (39½ in.)	105 cm (41½ in.)	110 cm (43½ in.)	115 cm (45½ in.)
BIAS BINDING: 4 CM (1½ IN.) WIDE, IN A LIGHT-WEIGHT COTTON	165 cm (65 in.)	170 cm (67 in.)	175 cm (69 in.)	180 cm (71 in.)	185 cm (73 in.)	190 cm (75 in.)	195 cm (77 in.)	200 cm (79 in.)	205 cm (81 in.)	210 cm (83 in.)
IRON-ON INTERFACING MEDIUM-WEIGHT	All sizes: 25 x 20 cm (10 x 8 in.) for all three welt pieces (D)									

ANNA WEARS A SHORTENED VERSION OF THE COMFORT PANTS IN A SIZE M, MADE USING TONE-ON-TONE BLACK COTTON SCRAPS.

PATTERN

This project is made using the Comfort Pants pattern with no changes. The pattern pieces required are outlined in the Layout Plans section below.

LAYOUT PLANS

This project is cut from patchwork fabric that you make yourself. The patchwork pieces required have been arranged in three separate layout plans (1, 2 and 3) to ensure you get the most efficient layout.

A: Front leg – 1 pair

B: Back leg – 1 pair

C: Waistband – 1

D: Pocket welt – 3

E: Front pocket facing – 1 pair

F: Front pocket lining – 1 pair

G: Back pocket facing – 1

H: Back pocket lining – 1

Note:

For layout plan 3 you can use one fabric offcut, as the pieces are quite small and work best without too many patchwork seams in them.

Layout plan 1

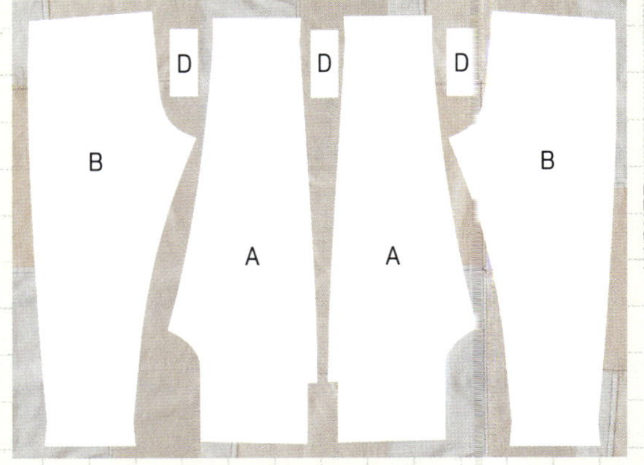

WIDTH

Layout plan 2

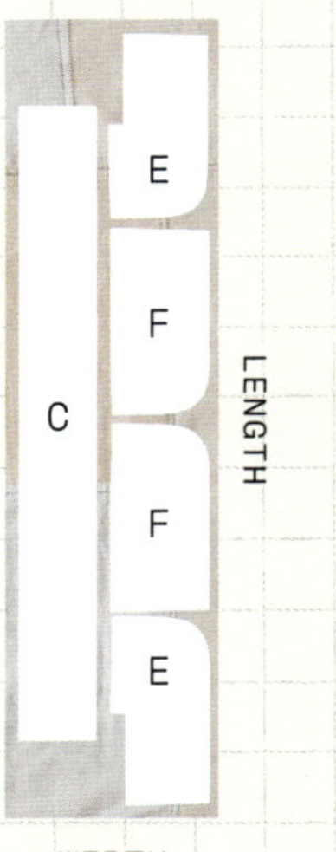

Layout plan 3

G

H

LENGTH

WIDTH

METHOD

PATCHWORK & CUTTING

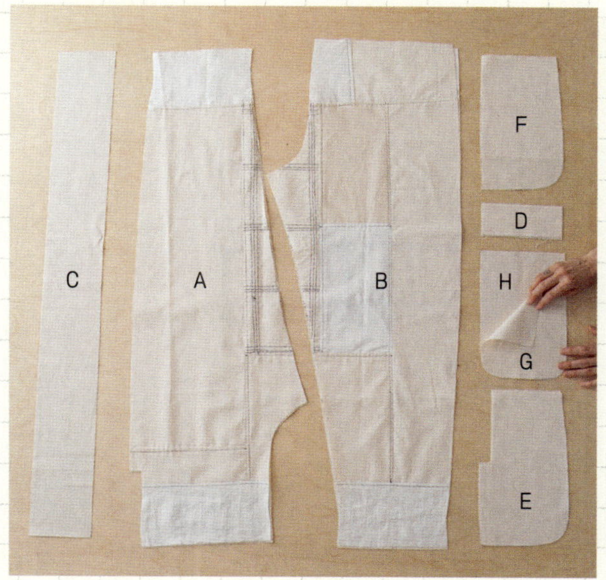

1. Patchwork together three different fabric sizes. To do this, start by laying out the required paper pattern pieces in your size, as shown in layout plans 1, 2 and 3. Measure the width and length to work out the total amount of fabric you need for each, allowing 2.5 cm (1 in.) extra all around.

2. Lay out and sew together your patchwork to the sizes required. You will need to overlap all of your patchwork pieces by 1.5 cm (⅝ in.) to allow for the total seam allowances needed for a raw felled seam. Sew the seams using a raw felled seam (see page 29).

3. Pin your paper patterns to the patchworked fabric, following layout plans 1, 2 and 3, and cut out all your patchwork pieces.

4. Apply medium-weight iron-on interfacing to the wrong side of the three pocket welts. Also apply a piece of interfacing the same size as the welt pattern piece to the wrong side of the back leg, where the welt pocket will be situated.

Note: All seam allowances are 1 cm (⅜ in.) unless otherwise stated.

SEWING

1. As soon as you have cut out all your pieces, secure the patchwork seams by topstitching about 8 mm (¼ in.) away from the raw edges so that the seams don't start to unravel.

2. Sew the side-seam welt pockets to the front legs (see page 32).

3. Sew the back welt pocket on the right back leg only (photo 3a); see page 34. Bind the raw edges of the pocket bag (photo 3b); see page 37.

4. With right sides together, sew the side seams of the front and back pants, making sure you neatly sew at the pocket welt section (see step 10 on page 33). Overlock the seams together and press towards to the back.

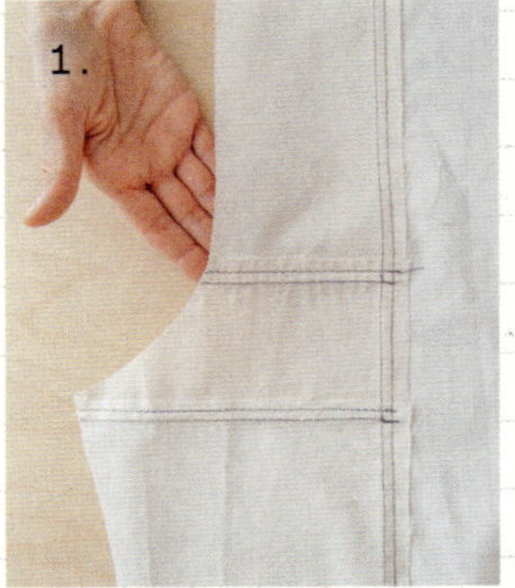

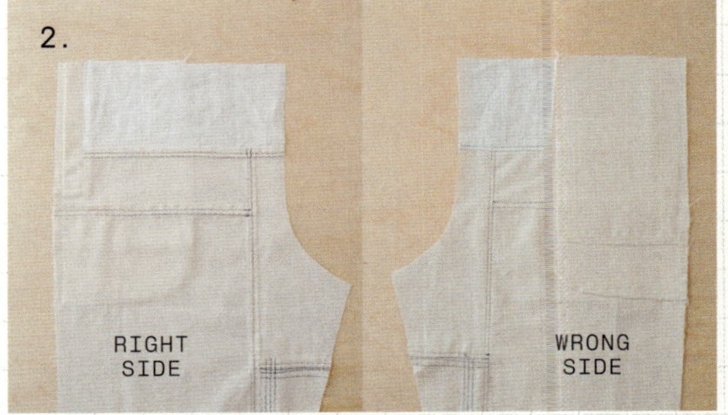

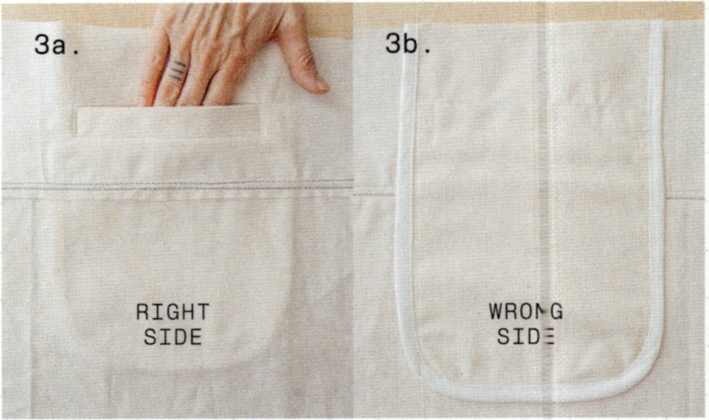

5. To sew the pleats in the front pieces, bring the two notches at the top of each front together, folding towards the side seams. Pin the pleats and the top of the pocket bag in place and pin the pocket bag to the top of the pants, making sure the welt butts up right against the side seam.

6. Topstitch across the top from the pleat to the side seam, making sure the pocket bag is secured neatly across the top and keeping your stitches within the seam allowance.

7. With right sides together, sew the centre front and centre back crotch seams, then overlock the seams together and press to one side.

8. With right sides together, sew the inside leg seams, matching the crotch seams together neatly. Overlock the seams together and press towards the back.

9. Attach a strip of binding to one long end of the waistband (see page 42). With right sides together, sew the centre back seam of the waistband, then press the seam open.

10. Attach the waistband and insert the elastic (see pages 42–43).

11. Turn the hem of each leg to the wrong side by 1 cm (⅜ in.) and press. Turn up the hem a second time as far as the notch. Pin in place and topstitch the hem through all layers, close to the fold line.

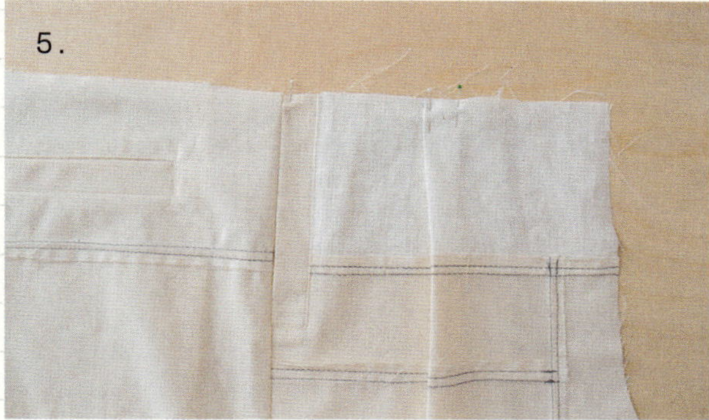

SHORT SHORTS

These shorts are based on the Comfort Pants pattern. We really wanted them to feel a little sporty, so they have curved sides and contrast binding to finish around all the hems and side seams, reminiscent of '70s jogging shorts. Sam loves a good pair of colourful short shorts and his favourite pair finally died at the end of this last summer, so we were super excited to come up with this new design. As you can see, this pair was made using lots of small patchwork rectangles. This particular method is quite time consuming, so short shorts seemed like a pretty achievable item to make. That said, if you have the patience this method would look so nice in many different garments. Imagine it in a pair of loose-fitting pants or even a relaxed shirt – hell, if you're really game why not go wild and try and make a twin set with it?!

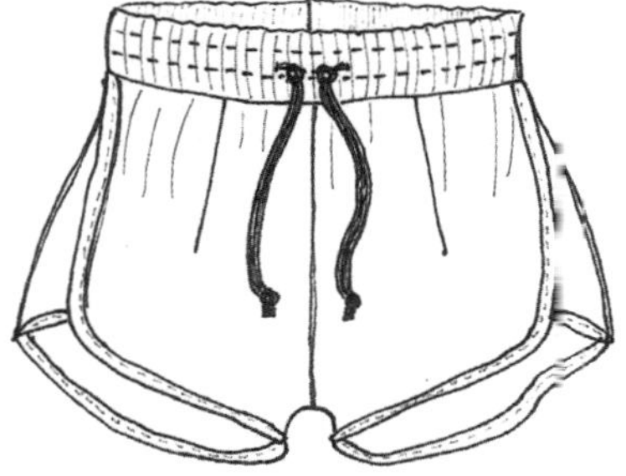

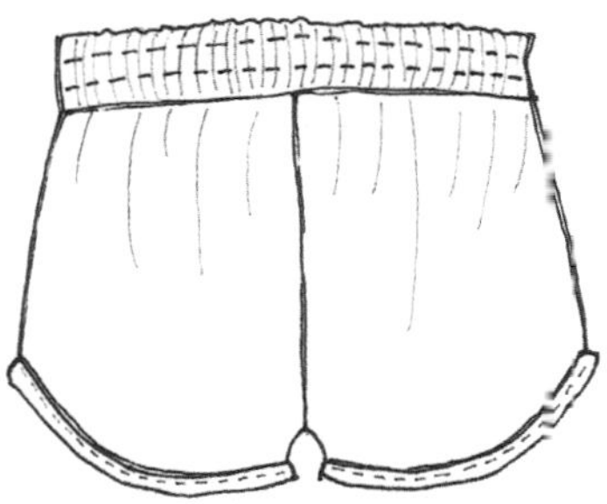

SKILL LEVEL ●●●○○

TECHNIQUES

Patchwork with zig-zag topstitching

SIZES MADE

Size M worn by Edith

FABRIC

Light- to medium-weight linen remnants. You can use quite small scraps for this patchwork as all the pieces are cut to a width of 5 cm (2 in.), with differing lengths based on the scraps you have. We just recommend not cutting pieces that are smaller than 5 x 5 cm (2 x 2 in.), as it gets too fiddly.

NOTIONS

	XS	S	M	L	XL	2XL	3XL	4XL	5XL	6XL
ELASTIC: 5 CM (2 IN.) WIDE	70 cm (27½ in.)	75 cm (29½ in.)	80 cm (31½ in.)	85 cm (33½ in.)	90 cm (35½ in.)	95 cm (37½ in.)	100 cm (39½ in.)	105 cm (41½ in.)	110 cm (43½ in.)	115 cm (45½ in.)
BIAS BINDING: 4 CM (1½ IN.) WIDE, IN A LIGHT-WEIGHT COTTON	300 cm (118 in.)	310 cm (122 in.)	320 cm (126 in.)	330 cm (130 in.)	340 cm (134 in.)	350 cm (138 in.)	360 cm (142 in.)	370 cm (146 in.)	380 cm (150 in.)	390 cm (154 in.)
BIAS STRIPS: 2.5CM (1 IN.) WIDE, FOR ROULEAU TIES	150 cm (59 in.)	155 cm (61 in.)	160 cm (63 in.)	165 cm (65 in.)	170 cm (67 in.)	175 cm (69 in.)	180 cm (71 in.)	185 cm (73 in.)	190 cm (75 in.)	195 cm (77 in.)
IRON-ON INTERFACING MEDIUM-WEIGHT	All sizes: 6 x 3 cm (2½ x 1¼ in.)									

PATTERN

The shorts are made using the Comfort Pants pattern pieces shown here. Use the 'Shorts' length and sides, as indicated on the pattern.

A: Front leg

B: Back leg

C: Waistband

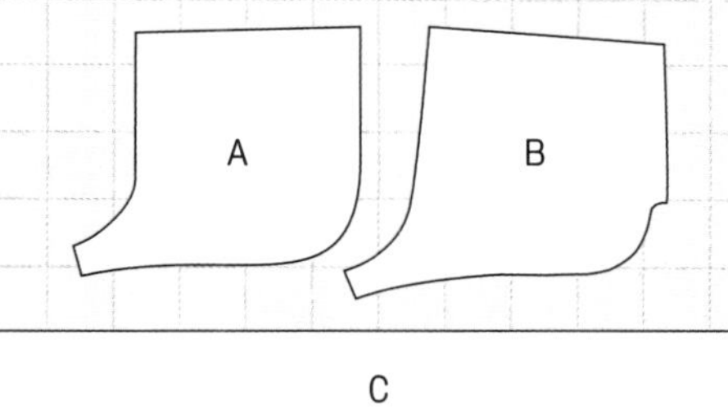

METHOD

PATCHWORK

For this project, it is easiest if you patchwork together pieces to the approximate size of the pattern pieces (see page 49). Using each pattern piece as a guide, work out the approximate width and length you need. For this project we patchworked one piece large enough for both the left and right front legs (so we could cut the legs on a double layer of fabric), one piece for both the left and right back legs, and one piece for the waistband.

1. Prepare your scraps by cutting out lots of 5-cm (2-in.) wide strips along a straight grain, either vertically or horizontally. Cut the strips into different-sized rectangles, anywhere from 5 to 10 cm (2 to 4 in.) long. With right sides together, taking a 6-mm (¼-in.) seam allowance, sew together enough strips to go along the length of the pattern pieces you are working with, allowing for a little extra top and bottom.

2. Make as many long strips as you need to cover the whole pattern piece, keeping in mind that when you join the strips vertically each one will have a seam allowance of around 6 mm (¼ in.), so you will lose that amount from each side of each strip.

3. Press all the seams to one side and zig-zag stitch across them, on the right side. This will add a nice detail and also cover the raw edges of the seams underneath, so that they do not fray.

4. Finally, taking a 6-mm (¼-in.) seam allowance, sew all the strips together along the vertical edges. Press the seams to one side and zig-zag across the seams to finish them as well. See page 51 for tips on how to sew together lots of very small strips.

CUTTING

Pin your paper patterns to the relevant patchworked fabric pieces and cut out.

- A: Front leg – cut 1 pair
- B: Back leg – cut 1 pair
- C: Waistband – cut 1

Note: All seam allowances are 1 cm (⅜ in.) unless otherwise stated.

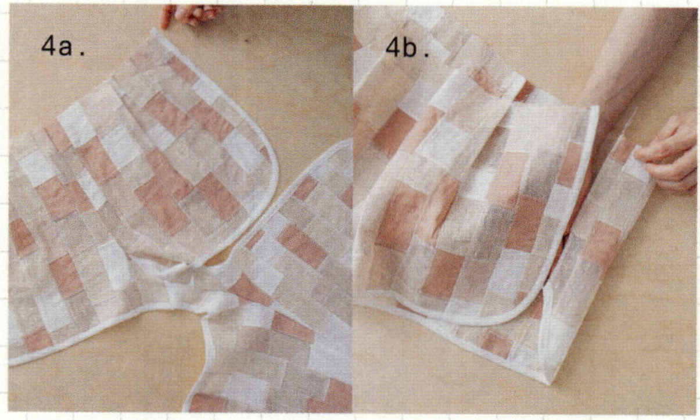

SEWING

1. With right sides together, sew the centre front and centre back seams. Overlock the seams together and press to one side, pressing the centre front and centre back seams in opposite directions to reduce bulk.

2. With right sides together, sew the inside leg seams. Overlock the inside leg seams together, then press towards the back.

3. Sew the pleats down across the top of the front waist, bringing the two notches at the top of each front together and folding towards the side seams. Topstitch across the top of the pleats to secure them neatly in place, keeping your stitches within the seam allowance.

4. Bind (see page 37) the front side seams and hems, finishing at the angled point on the back side seam (photo 4a). Overlock the raw edge of the back side seam (photo 4b).

5. Overlap the front side seam over the back side seam by approximately 2 cm (¾ in.), then pin in place and work a line of topstitching down each edge of the binding. Secure with some extra stitches at the finished point.

6. Find the centre point of your waistband and fold it in half, right sides together. Measure 2.5 cm (1 in.) down from the fold and mark one buttonhole each side of the centre point. They should each be 1.5 cm (⅝ in.) wide and be placed 1.5 cm (⅝ in.) apart; you may need to tweak the placement slightly to make sure they do not cross over any thick zig-zag seams.

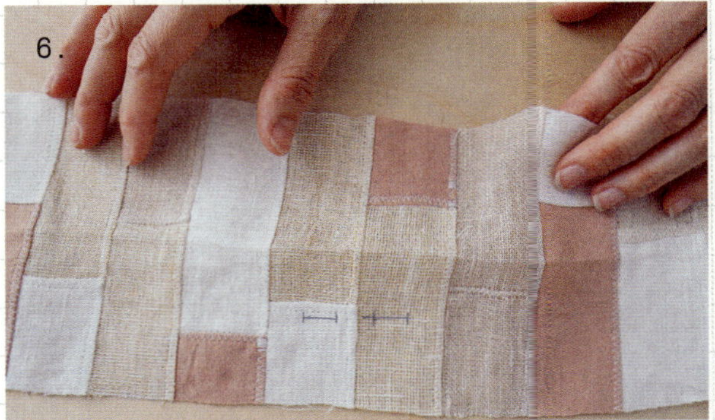
6.

7. Apply a small piece of iron-on interfacing to the wrong side to make the buttonholes stronger. Sew the buttonholes and cut them open (see page 30).

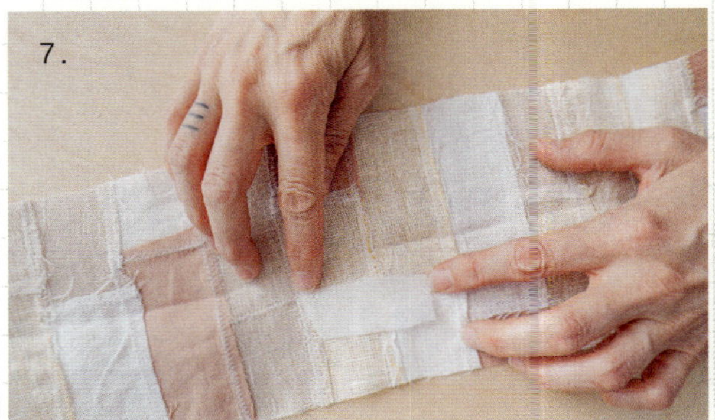
7.

8. Attach bias binding to the other raw edge of the waistband (away from the buttonholes). With right sides together, sew the centre back seam of the waistband, then press the seam open. Attach the waistband to the shorts and insert the elastic (see pages 42–43).

8.

9. Work two rows of stitching all around the waistband – one above the buttonholes and one below – to create a channel for the rouleau tie. Stretch the waistband out as you go.

10. Sew the rouleau tie and turn it right side out (see page 30). Using a safety pin, thread the tie through the waistband by taking it in through one of the buttonholes at the front and bringing it out through the other. Tie a knot at each end of the tie and trim away the excess.

10.

PATCHWORK TEE

This tee is patchworked together using lots of little leftover jersey pieces we had saved from other jobs, and also little sample swatches we had collected from different suppliers over the years.

You can achieve the same look by cutting up leftover jerseys into squares and rectangles.

Like many of the projects in this book, you could make your garment more subtle by using tone-on-tone fabrics. We chose to use the exposed overlocked seams on the outside of the garment, because we loved the extra texture – plus it's super playful and light hearted. You can just as easily have the overlocked seams on the inside if you prefer. Patchworking stretch fabrics together can be a little fiddly, so practise on some scraps first – but don't be too fussy about making every seam perfect! It will all even out in the wash, as they say.

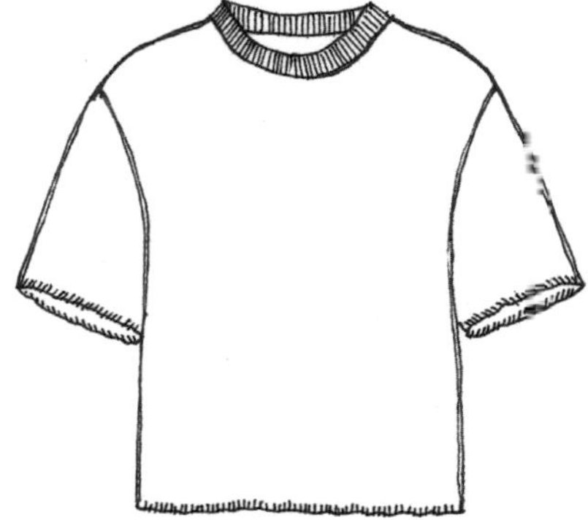

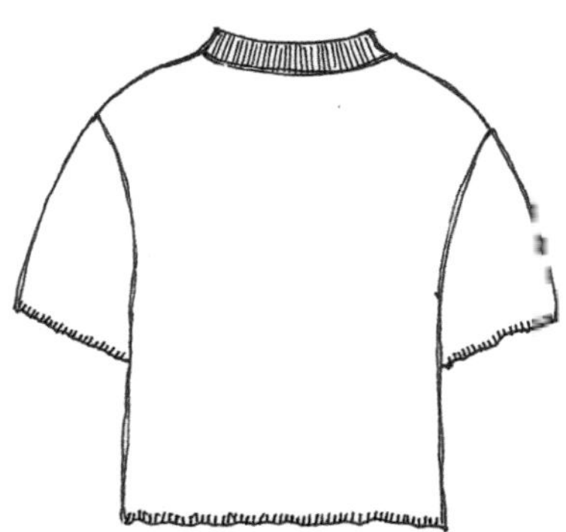

SKILL LEVEL ●●○○○

TECHNIQUES

Patchwork

Exposed overlocked seams on stretch fabric

SIZES MADE

Size L/XL worn by Shoko (who was 7 months pregnant at the time of taking these photos!)

FABRIC

Cotton jersey offcuts. For the neckband, we used a 2 x 1 organic cotton ribbing with a small amount of elastane in it.

NOTIONS

N/A

PATTERN

The Patchwork Tee is made using the Tee pattern. We wanted it to look a little oversized, cropped and boxy, so we removed 13 cm (5 in.) from the hem of the pattern and also used the pattern two sizes bigger (Shoko is normally a size S/M and we used the L/XL pattern), but you can adjust it to your own preference, if you wish to adjust it at all.

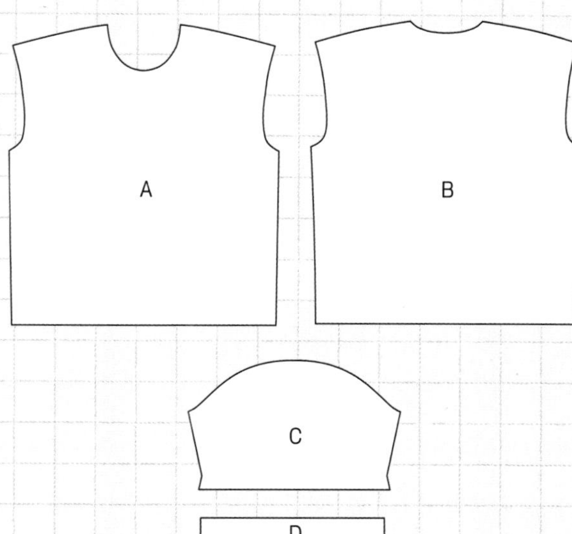

A: Front

B: Back

C: Sleeve

D: Neckband

METHOD

PATCHWORK

For this project, it is easiest if you patchwork together pieces to the approximate size of the pattern pieces for the front, back and sleeves (see page 49). Using each pattern piece as a guide, work out the approximate width and length you need.

1. Start planning out your patchwork pieces. We broke up our sections a little bit so as not to make it too overwhelming, making four sections for each individual pattern piece (including the bodies and the sleeves) and breaking them up into alternating coloured and neutral sections. As an example, for our front body we did a colour section with small scraps for the bottom left and top right sections, and more neutral scraps in larger pieces for the bottom right and top left.

2. Now you can start to sew your patchwork pieces together by planning sections out into units, as explained on pages 49–50. Here we show an example of the patchwork we made for the front body. We started by sewing together, in various stages, the four different units (photo 2a). Then we joined the coloured units to the neutral units (photo 2b), and finally we joined these units together down the centre (photo 2c). Sew the seams using a 3- or 4-thread overlocker. If you want the seams to be exposed, then make sure you sew your pieces wrong sides together.

2a.

2b.

2c.

Tip: Try to cut the patchwork pieces along the grain as much as possible (the stretch can go in either direction).

Note: If you don't have an overlocker, you could use zig-zag stitch and a ballpoint needle instead – but sew the pieces right sides together, so that the seams are on the inside of the garment, otherwise it could look a bit messy.

CUTTING

Pin your paper patterns to the relevant patchworked fabric pieces and cut out. We cut all of our pieces on the fold, as this helps to keep them symmetrical. The neckband is cut in ribbing.

Patchwork

- A: Front – cut 1
- B: Back – cut 1
- C: Sleeve – cut 1 pair

Ribbing

- D: Neckband – cut 1

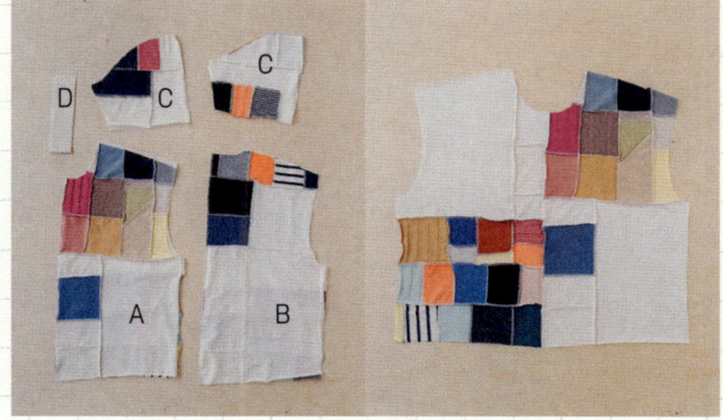

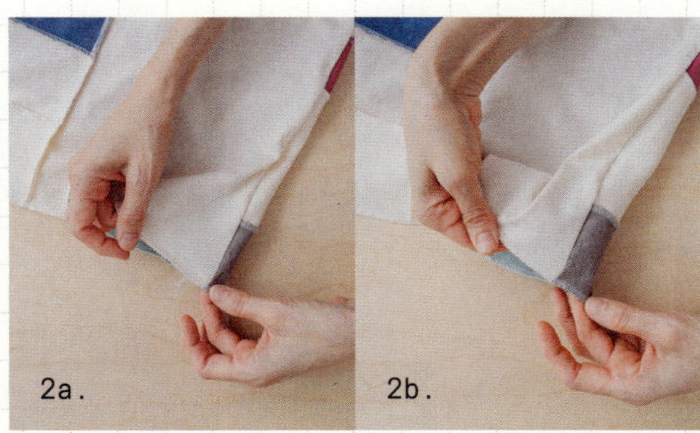

SEWING

1. Follow steps 1–6 of the Logo Tee project, page 172, to sew the shoulders, side seams, sleeves and neckband. When constructing the garment, we sewed the seams with the overlocking on the inside (as opposed to the exposed seams used for the patchwork). This is to differentiate between the patchwork as its own 'fabric' and the sewing of the tee as a garment.

2. In order to match the rest of the garment, we finished the hems using a 4-thread overlocker. Start on one side seam and run over the overlocking slightly at the end, leaving a small tail of overlocking (photo 2a). Tuck under the overlocking neatly and hand stitch it in place so that it doesn't show (photo 2b). Alternatively, you can turn up a small amount of the hem and sew it down with zig-zag stitching or a double row of stitching using a twin needle.

RE-MAKE JACKET

This re-make project uses a vintage Levi denim jacket. These types of jackets are very classic but the fit can tend to be quite dated and small in the body, so we wanted to try to make it more wearable and modern. We did this by adding a side-seam insert and adding a hem-band extension to make the sizing larger in the body, as well as replacing the original sleeves with wider and longer patchworked sleeves. (We used some of the fabric from the original sleeves for the Re-make Jeans on page 162, so nothing went to waste!)

The fabrics used for the patchwork are a mixture of denim offcuts from the original sleeves plus a selection of linen and cotton scraps. We also covered some stains with patches and mended a broken collar with patching in the same way. After having made this jacket, we left it in our shop on a Saturday to see if people were drawn to it. Every single person went straight to it and asked about it, so we will certainly be making more like this in the future! These instructions have some good fundamental techniques in adjusting and re-designing an existing garment. We see this project as inspiration to encourage you to make a unique re-make of your own.

SKILL LEVEL ●●●○○

TECHNIQUES

Patchwork

Hand quilting

RE-MAKE GARMENT USED

Vintage Levi jacket, labelled as a size L but it is very snug and fits more like a size S. After adjustments, the jacket is more like an actual size L, worn by Sarah.

FABRIC

For the patchwork we used a variety of light- to medium-weight cotton and linen scraps, all cut into even-sized squares measuring 7 x 7 cm (2¾ x 2¾ in.), giving a finished size of 5 x 5 cm (2 x 2 in.) once the seam allowance is taken away.

NOTIONS

- Cotton wadding to place under the patchwork pieces; the amount needed varies depending on the rework you are doing. We used it for the sleeves and side-seam inserts.
- Silky viscose to line the side-seam inserts and sleeves.

7CM (2¾ IN.)

RE-MAKE JACKET
PATCHWORK TEMPLATE

7CM (2¾ IN.)

METHOD

PREPARING THE JACKET

Prepare your garment for re-make. For this garment we unpicked the side and underarm seams and completely removed the sleeves. We also unpicked a section of the waistband along the side seams and all the way around the back. Once you've unpicked the sleeves, press them neatly so that the whole piece is nice and flat.

SIDE-SEAM INSERT

MAKING THE PATTERN PIECES

We made our own pattern pieces for the changes we wanted to implement: side seam insert, outer sleeve, sleeve lining and back hem-band extension.

SIDE-SEAM INSERT

The side-seam insert adds extra width around the waist and hips. This is the total width that we want to add at the underarm and hem, plus seam allowances; the length of the piece should match the length of the original jacket side seams, including seam allowance (see photo, top right).

OUTER SLEEVE

OUTER SLEEVE

As we are making changes to the width of the garment, we also need to add this into the sleeve width; each side of the sleeve head should have half the total extra width that has been added into the side seam of the body. For example, ifyou are adding a side-seam panel that is 5 cm (2 in.) wide at the top (underarm), then the sleeve head should be extended out on each side by 2.5 cm (1 in.).

On our pattern pieces, we also added an extra 1 cm (⅜ in.) for seam allowances wherever necessary. We used the sleeve head of the original garment as a guide and then made the top of the sleeve a mirrored piece (in other words, the front and back sides of the curve are the same, symmetrical). We also adjusted the rest of the sleeve to be both wider and longer. We added a hem turn-up to the bottom of the sleeve of 5 cm (2 in.) and angled the side seam accordingly at the fold-up point (as shown right).

SLEEVE LINING

For the sleeve lining, we traced the new outer sleeve pattern onto a separate piece of paper and then made the necessary changes. The lining is 5 cm (2 in.) shorter in length than the outer sleeve and the lining hem width is extended out slightly to match the width of the outer sleeve hem, as these pieces will be sewn together.

BACK HEM-BAND EXTENSION

This piece should be the same height as the original band. The width is based on the width added into the body – so for this jacket we made a hem band that is 10 cm (4 in.) wide plus seam allowance. Keep in mind that on these sorts of denim jackets the hem bands are often eased on a bit, so don't make your band too wide – allow for some ease on the jacket part.

1.

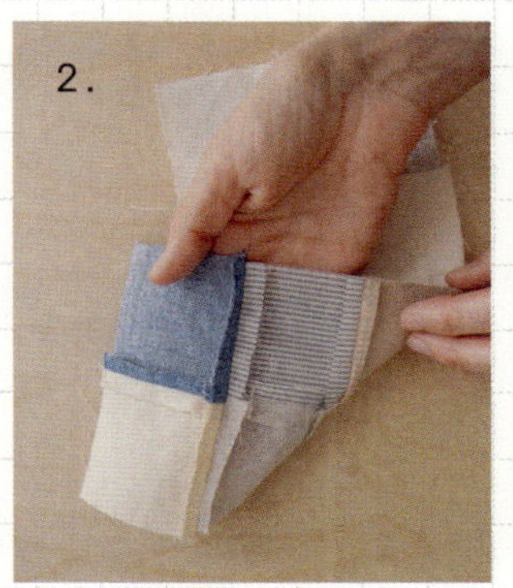

2.

CUTTING

Pin your new paper patterns to the relevant fabric(s) and cut out.

- Side-seam insert: cut 1 pair in wadding, 1 pair in lining fabric
- Outer sleeve: cut 1 pair in wadding
- Sleeve lining: cut 1 pair in lining fabric
- Back hem-band extension: cut 1 in wadding

PATCHWORK

For this project, it is easiest if you patchwork pieces together to the approximate size of the pattern pieces (see page 49). We used the cut wadding pieces as a guide for how big to make the patchwork.

1. We cut all our patchwork pieces into 7 x 7 cm (2¾ x 2¾ in.) squares and then laid them out across the sleeve outer wadding pieces, side-seam inserts and back hem-band extension.

2. Patchwork the squares together in horizontal strips first, using straight stitch and a 1-cm (⅜-in.) seam allowance, and then press the seams open. Join the rows together.

3. Pin the wadding pieces to the patchwork to use as a guide, then cut the patchwork pieces to the same size.

> Note: All seam allowances are 1 cm (⅜ in.) unless otherwise stated.

SEWING

1. Once the patchwork pieces were complete, we attached them to the wadding bases by straight stitching all around, 8 mm (¼ in.) away from the raw edges, to stop the seams of the patchwork from unravelling.

2. As a detail, we hand quilted the patchwork to the wadding by working a line of running stitch through all layers around the inner edge of every square, about 8 mm (¼ in.) away from the seams.

3. With right sides together, we sewed the side-seam inserts to the front and back side seams.

4. Next we attached the lining to the front side seam only.

5. Then we pressed the lining towards the back to cover the entire side-seam insert. We pressed the other end of the lining to the wrong side by 1 cm (⅜ in.), then hand tacked it in place to cover the back side seam.

6. With right sides together, we sewed the underarm seams of the outer sleeves and pressed the seams open. Then we did the same with the underarm seams of the sleeve lining pieces – although, if you have a fabric that frays quite easily, you might also want to secure the raw edges with an overlock or zig-zag stitch.

2.

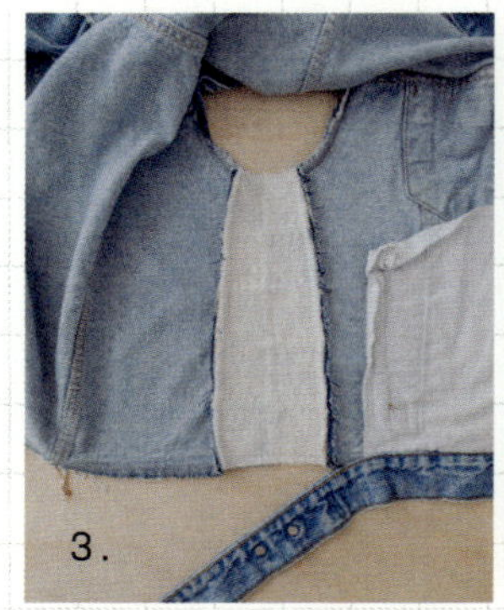

3.

4.

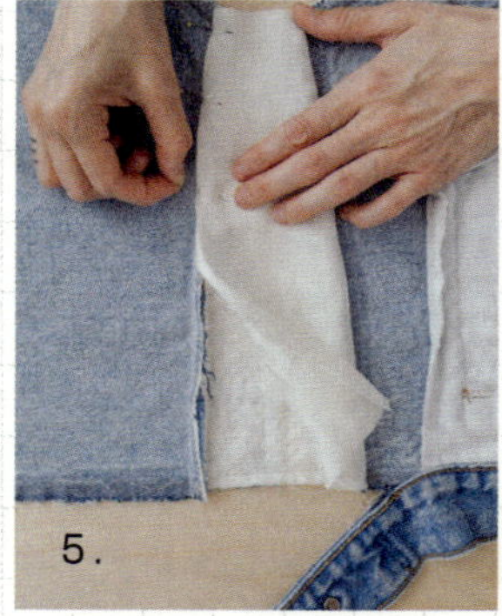

5.

7. With right sides together, we sewed the outer sleeve and sleeve lining pieces together at the sleeve hems (photo 7a). Then we pulled the sleeve lining up over the sleeve, wrong sides together, and pinned the sleeve heads of the outer sleeve and lining together. We secured the two layers of the sleeve head by stitching around it, about 8 mm (¼ in.) away from the raw edge (photo 7b).

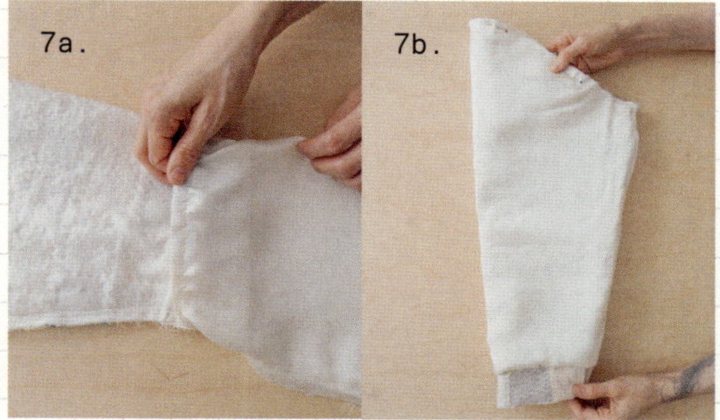
7a. 7b.

8. We pressed the sleeve hem up to the finished length and hand stitched it from the inside, close to the seam where the lining is joined.

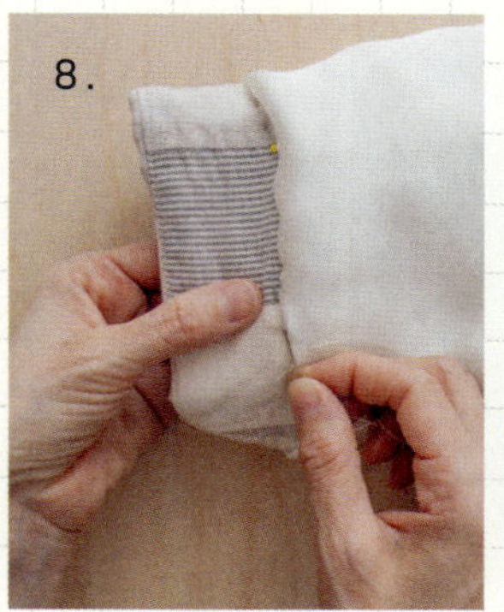
8.

9. With right sides together, we inserted the sleeve heads into the armholes and sewed them in place. We overlocked the seam allowances together and pressed the seams up into the shoulder (as this is where the bulk of the seams wanted to go).

9.

10. We then cut the original waistband apart at the centre back point and opened out the ends. With right sides together, we attached the waistband extension piece to the original waistband and pressed the seams open. Finally we folded the waistband in half, wrong sides together (so that the patchwork faced out on both sides), and stitched it back onto the hem, as on the original garment.

11. We finished off by adding some little patchwork squares over some stains and also mended one side of the collar that was damaged.

11.

WORKWEAR JACKET

We love the 'workwear' style! For us, it ticks all the boxes of what makes functional and comfortable garments. Its practical and timeless aesthetic can be dressed up or down, and garments are generally crafted with durability and longevity in mind.
This workwear jacket was one of the first patterns we ever created back in 2018. It has gone through many incarnations to get to the stage it is at now and we're both really happy with it. It has a relaxed fit, two patch pockets on the hip and one on the chest, as well as a straight blunt hem. It also has some lovely binding details on the facings and sleeve splits, which really make the finished garment something special. If you are going to patchwork together heavier fabrics, as we have done here, then it is a good idea to keep your patches on the large side to reduce the bulk. Enjoy!

SKILL LEVEL 

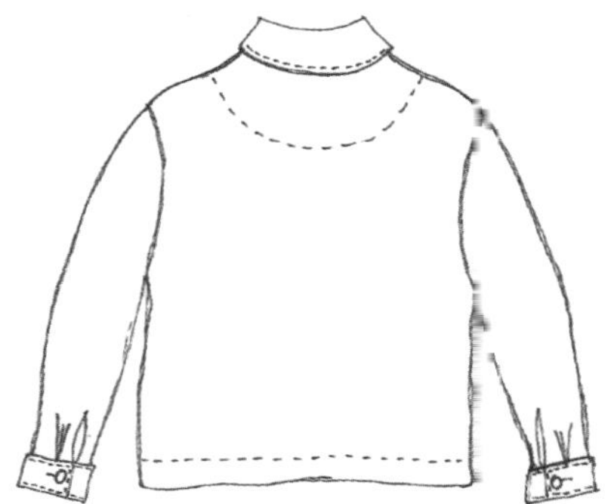

TECHNIQUES

Patchwork

SIZE MADE

S/M worn by Edith

FABRIC

Medium- to heavy-weight cotton and denim fabric offcuts. We recommend choosing either only dark colours or only light colours, as dark-coloured fabrics (and in particular darker denim colours) can bleed into the lighter ones when the garment is washed.

NOTIONS

	XS/S	S/M	M/L	L/XL	XL/2XL	2XL/3XL	3XL/4XL	4XL/5XL	5XL/6XL
BIAS BINDING: 4 CM (1½ IN.) WIDE, IN A LIGHT-WEIGHT COTTON	290 cm (114 in.)	300 cm (118 in.)	310 cm (122 in.)	320 cm (126 in.)	330 cm (130 in.)	340 cm (134 in.)	350 cm (138 in.)	360 cm (142 in.)	370 cm (146 in.)
IRON-ON INTERFACING MEDIUM-WEIGHT	FOR FRONT AND BACK FACINGS AND ONE COLLAR PIECE All sizes: approx. 60 x 115 cm (24 x 46 in.)								
BUTTONS	FOR FRONT AND SLEEVE CUFFS All sizes: six, each 25 mm (1 in.)								

PATTERN

This project is made using the Workwear Jacket pattern, with no changes. The pattern pieces required are outlined in the Layout Plans section.

LAYOUT PLANS

This project is cut from patchwork fabric that you make yourself. The patchwork pieces required have been arranged in three separate cutting plans (1, 2 and 3) to ensure you get the most efficient layout. The sleeve-split binding and neck loop are cut from light-weight cotton.

Layout plans 1, 2 and 3: patchwork fabric

- A: Front body – 1 pair
- B: Back body – 1
- C: Workwear sleeve – 1 pair
- D: Front facing – 1 pair
- E: Back facing – 1
- F: Workwear collar – 1 pair
- G: Sleeve cuff – 1 pair
- I: Chest pocket – 1
- J: Hip pocket – 1 pair

Layout plan: light-weight cotton

- H: Sleeve-split binding
- K: Neck loop

Patchwork fabric

Layout plan 1

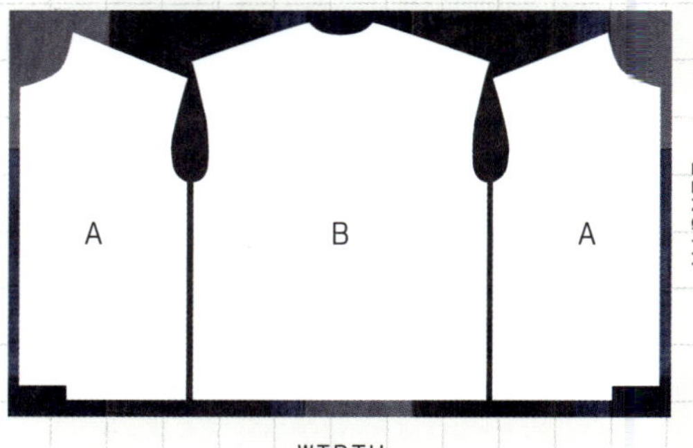

Layout plan 2

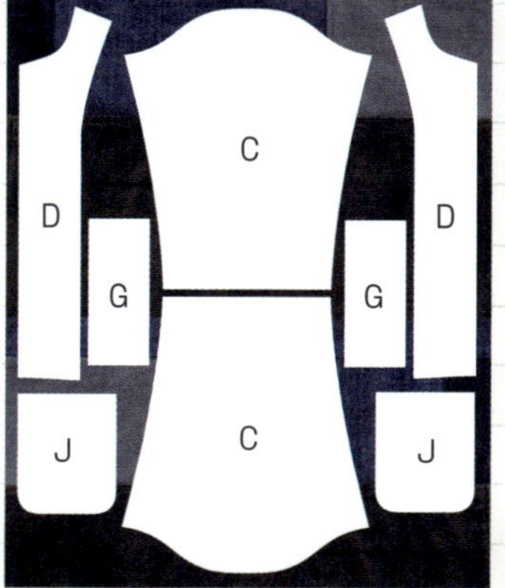

Layout plan 3

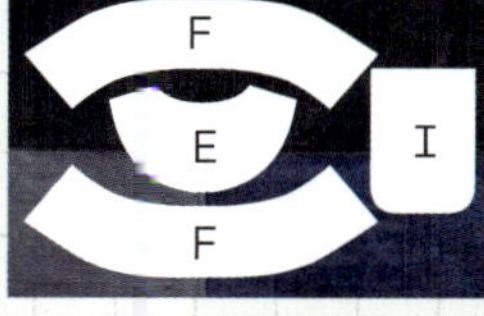

Light-weight cotton

METHOD

PATCHWORK

1. Patchwork together three different fabric sizes. To do this, start by laying out the required paper pattern pieces in your size, as shown in layout plans 1, 2 and 3. Measure the width and length to work out the total amount of fabric you need for each, allowing 2.5 cm (1 in.) extra all around.

2. Lay out and sew together your patchwork to the sizes required. You will need to overlap all of your patchwork pieces by 2 cm (¾ in.), to allow for a seam allowance of 1 cm (⅜ in.). Sew the seams using the Stitch and Overlock method (see page 52): overlock the seam allowances together, press to one side, then topstitch all seam allowances down around 8 mm (¼ in.) away from the seam.

CUTTING

1. Cut out all your patchwork pieces following layout plans 1, 2 and 3.
2. Cut the back neck loop and sleeve-split binding pieces from light-weight cotton to reduce bulk.
3. Apply medium-weight iron-on interfacing to the wrong side of the front (D) and back (E) facings and one collar piece (F).

Note: All seam allowances are 1 cm (⅜ in.) unless otherwise stated.

SEWING

1. As soon as you have cut out all your pieces, secure the patchwork seams by topstitching about 8 mm (¼ in.) away from the raw edges so that the seams don't start to unravel.

2. Place the front and back body pieces (A and B) right sides together and sew the shoulder seams. Overlock the seam allowances together and press towards the back.

3. With right sides together, insert the sleeve heads into the armholes, making sure you match the shoulder notch on the sleeves to the shoulder seams on the body and that the sleeve split is positioned at the back. Sew in place, overlock the seam allowances together and press the seam allowances down into the sleeves.

4. With right sides together, sew the underarm and body side seams together in one continuous line of stitching on each side. Overlock the seam allowances together and press towards the back.

5. With right sides together, sew the front and back facings together at the shoulders. Press the seams open. Bind the outer edges of the facings all the way around (see pages 37 and 40).

6. Sew the collar together and then attach it to the neck of the jacket (see page 39). With right sides together, pin the facing around the neck of the body, sandwiching the collar in between. Stitch in place, then stitch along the centre front edges to attach the facings to the body of the jacket all the way down. Open out the facings and press the seam allowances towards the facings.

7. Bind the hem along the longest part of the hem all the way around (but not including the cut-out sections at the fronts) – see page 37.

8. With right sides together, fold the facings back onto the jacket front along the cut-out section. Sew along the bottom edge. Bag out, then press the rest of the hem up as far as the notch and pin in place. Topstitch the hems and facings down all the way around (see page 41).

9. Now make and attach the neck loop (photo 9a): Fold the long ends of the fabric to the wrong side by 1 cm (⅜ in.) and press (photo 9b), then fold the loop in half, press and pin in place. Edge stitch close to each long edge (photo 9c).

10. Press in each end of the loop to the wrong side by 1 cm (⅜ in.) and then place at the very centre of the back neck, on the wrong side of the garment. Work two rows of topstitching across the short ends of the loop on each side, through all layers.

11. Attach the sleeve-split bindings, sew the pleat in the sleeves and attach the hem cuffs (see pages 37–38).

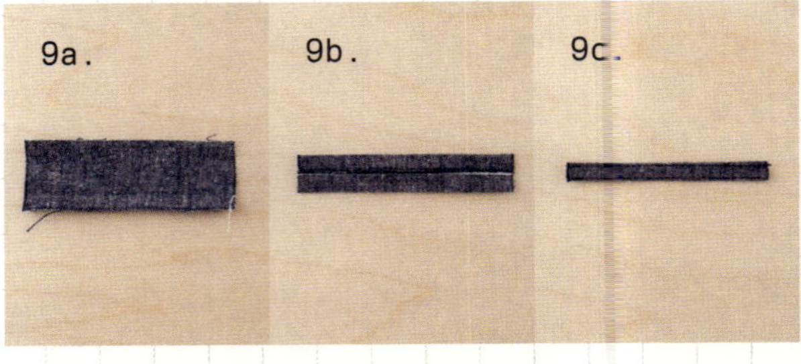

Tip: The placement of the pockets is a matter of personal preference, but we find that the chest pocket looks nice with the top edge starting around 23–25 cm (9–10 in.) down from the shoulder. The bottom edges of the hip pockets should start around 5 cm (2 in.) up from the finished hem. Both chest and hip pockets should start 8.5 cm (3½ in.) away from the centre front edges.

Tip: The first horizontal buttonhole on the jacket front should be placed about 2.5 cm (1 in.) down from the top, with three more buttonholes spaced about 15 cm (6 in.) apart below it. For the cuffs, centre the button and buttonhole to the height of the cuff, with the start of each buttonhole and the centre of each button positioned 2.5 cm (1 in.) away from the edge.

12.

12. Prepare the patch pockets, then pin them in place on the jacket and topstitch down through all layers, including the facings, as this helps to hold these down (see page 37).

13.

13. Sew buttons and horizontal buttonholes on the centre fronts and sleeve cuffs (see the tip above).

QUILTED COAT

Ever since Birgitta did her first run of 'Blanket Coats' (made using vintage wool blankets) for her self-titled label back in Melbourne in 2014, coat-making season has been a time of year we love – it takes the sting out of the impending winter! This coat is a really timeless shape – it's essentially a quilted trench. It takes a lot of work, but it is well worth the effort – and when you're finished, you should have an heirloom piece that will serve you for ever.

We have incorporated some lovely welt pockets into this coat, which are definitely for quite experienced sewers. If this is too scary, you can do patch pockets instead; either way, they will look great! We made two variations of this coat. The colourful and checked one worn by Shoko is a real statement piece, as the eye gets drawn to a mass of differing shapes, patterns and colours. If this isn't your style, try a version that is patchworked together with tone-on-tone neutral colours, much like the denim one worn by Edith. Either way, don't let this project intimidate you!

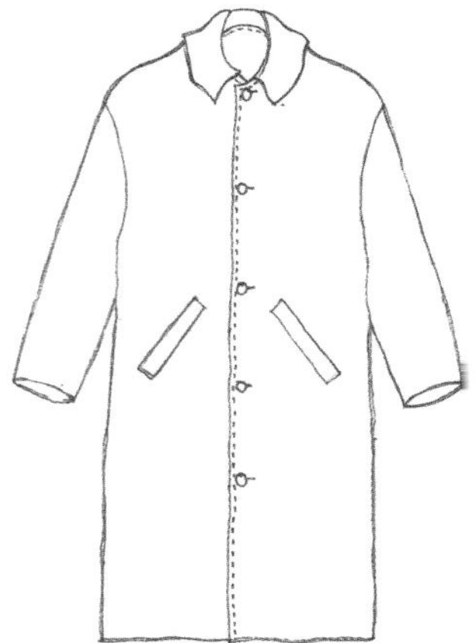

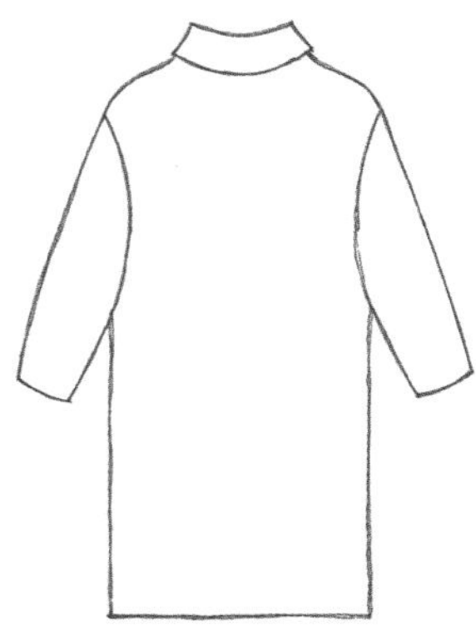

SKILL LEVEL ●●●●●

TECHNIQUES

Patchwork

Quilting

SIZE MADE

S/M worn by Shoko, S/M worn by Edith

FABRIC

The outer fabric has been patchworked together using offcuts of light- to medium-weight cotton fabrics, and wadding the same size has been added to the underside of the patchwork fabric. The wadding is an organic cotton/recycled poly blend. Light-to medium-weight cotton is used for the lining.

NOTIONS

	XS/S	S/M	M/L	L/XL	XL/2XL	2XL/3XL	3XL/4XL	4XL/5XL	5XL/6XL
BIAS BINDING: 4 CM (1½ IN.) WIDE, IN A LIGHT-WEIGHT COTTON	265 cm (104 in.)	270 cm (106 in.)	275 cm (108 in.)	280 cm (110 in.)	285 cm (112 in.)	290 cm (114 in.)	295 cm (116 in.)	300 cm (118 in.)	305 cm (120 in.)
BUTTONS	FOR FRONT All sizes: five, each 20–25 mm (¾–1 in.)								

PATTERN

The Quilted Coat is made using the Workwear Jacket pattern. The pattern pieces and adjustments required are outlined here:

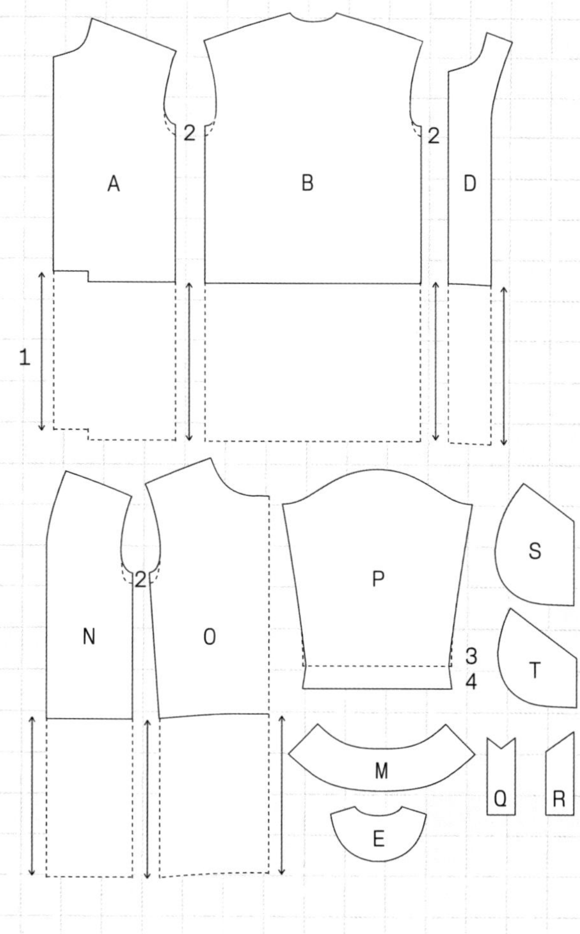

Pattern pieces

- A: Front body
- B: Back body
- D: Front facing
- E: Back facing
- M: Coat collar
- Q: Pocket welt
- R: Pocket facing
- P: Coat sleeve
- N: Front lining
- O: Back lining
- S: Pocket underlining
- T: Pocket top lining

Pattern adjustments

1. Lengthen pattern pieces A, B, D, N and O by 45 cm (17¾ in.) – retain the original shape of the hem.
2. On pattern pieces A, B, D, N and O, follow the line marked for the coat armhole.
3. For the sleeve lining: on pattern piece P, follow the line marked for the sleeve lining.
4. For the outer sleeve: on pattern piece P, follow the line marked for the outer sleeve.

LAYOUT PLANS

The outer coat is cut from quilted patchwork fabric that you make yourself. All the required pattern pieces have been arranged in several layouts showing the most efficient way both to prepare your patchwork fabric and to cut the pattern pieces. Layout plans 1, 2 and 3 are for the outer quilted patchwork fabric, while layout plans 4 and 5 are for the lining pieces. (We patchworked together our own lining using large pieces of light-weight cotton fabrics, but you can re-arrange your layout a little and cut this from fabric from the roll if you prefer.)

LAYOUT PLANS 1, 2 AND 3: QUILTED PATCHWORK FABRIC

- A: Front body – 1 pair
- B: Back body – 1
- D: Front facing – 1 pair
- E: Back facing – 1
- P: Coat sleeve (outer) – 1 pair
- M: Coat collar – 1 pair
- Q: Pocket welt – 1 pair
- R: Pocket facing – 1 pair

LAYOUT PLANS 4 AND 5: LINING FABRIC

- P: Coat sleeve (lining) – 1 pair
- N: Front lining – 1 pair
- O: Back lining – 1 pair
- S: Pocket underlining – 1 pair
- T: Pocket top lining – 1 pair

Patchwork fabric

Layout plan 1

A B A
LENGTH
WIDTH

Layout plan 2

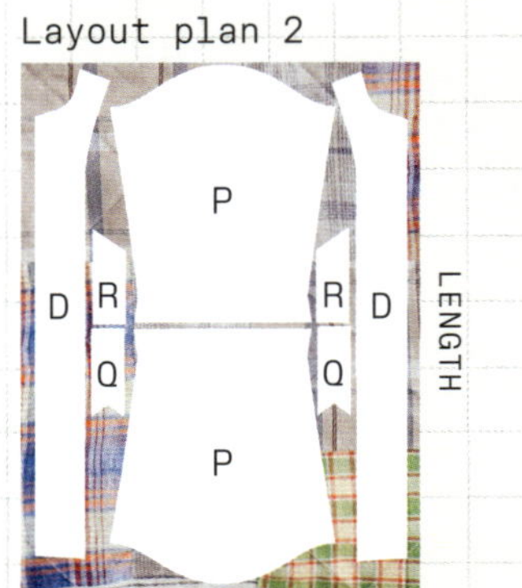

WIDTH

Layout plan 3

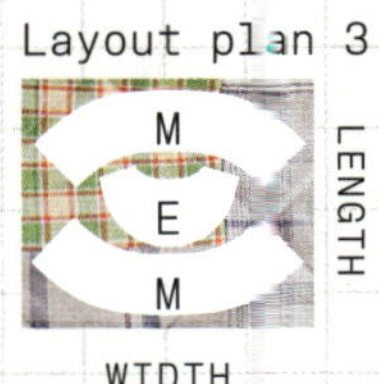

WIDTH

Lining fabric

Layout plan 4

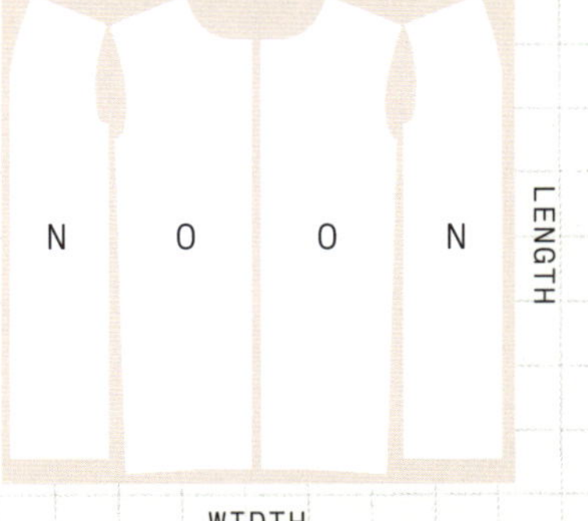

WIDTH

Layout plan 5

S P P S
T T
LENGTH
WIDTH

METHOD

PATCHWORK

1. Patchwork together three different fabric sizes. To do this, start by laying out the required paper pattern pieces in your size, as shown in layout plans 1, 2 and 3. Measure the width and length to work out the total amount of fabric you need for each, allowing 2.5 cm (1 in.) extra all around.

2. Lay out and sew together your patchwork to the sizes required. You will need to overlap all of your patchwork pieces by 2 cm (¾ in.), to allow for a total seam allowance of 1 cm (⅜ in.) – see page 49. Sew the seams using straight stitch, then press the seams open to reduce bulk (see page 53).

3. Repeat the patchwork process for the lining pieces, following layout plans 4 and 5. Alternatively, cut your lining pieces using fabric off the roll.

QUILTING

Place a layer of wadding the same size on the wrong side of the three patchwork fabric blocks. Machine quilt all three patchwork blocks (see page 31). We spaced our quilting lines 12 cm (4¾ in.) apart.

CUTTING

Pin your paper patterns to the relevant fabric, following layout plans 1, 2 and 3 for the pieces that you need to cut in quilted patchwork fabric and layout plans 4 and 5 for the pieces that you need to cut in lining fabric. Cut out.

Note: All seam allowances are 1 cm (⅜ in.) unless otherwise stated.

SEWING

1. As soon as you have cut out all your pieces, secure patchwork seams by topstitching about 8 mm (¼ in.) away from the raw edges so that seams don't start to unravel.

2. Sew the angled welt pockets into the front body pieces (see page 36), following the placement dots on the pattern.

3. Place the front and back outer body pieces right sides together and sew the shoulder seams. Press the seams open.

4. With right sides together, insert the outer sleeves into the armholes, making sure you match the shoulder notch on the sleeves to the shoulder seams on the body. Sew in place. Press the seam allowances down into the sleeves.

5. With right sides together, sew the underarm and body side seams together in one continuous line of stitching on each side. Press the seam allowances open.

6. With right sides together, sew the front and back facings together at the shoulders. Press the seams open.

7. Bind the outer raw edges of the front and back facings all the way around, hem to hem (see pages 37 and 40).

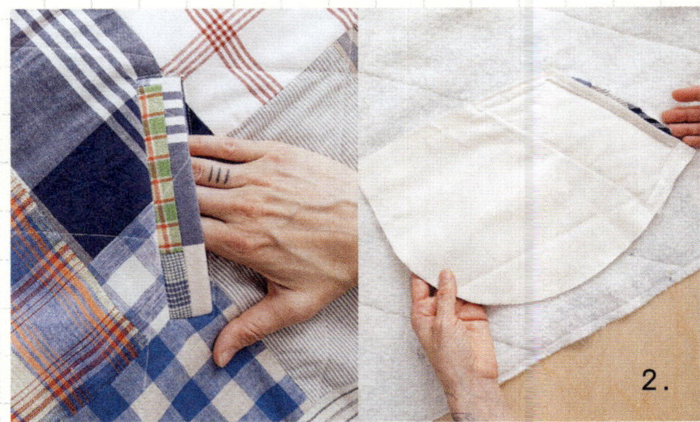

2.

Tip: It's a good idea to hold up the front body against yourself to double check where the pockets sit on you.

8. Sew the collar pieces together and turn right side out (see page 39). The underside (lining) of the collar should extend past the top layer, as shown here, due to the understitching. This ensures that the lining of the collar will not roll out and become visible when it is attached to the coat. Attach the collar to the neck of the coat (see page 39).

9. With right sides together, pin the facing around the neck of the body, sandwiching the collar in between. Stitch in place, then stitch along the centre front edges to attach the facings to the body of the jacket all the way down (see page 40). Open out the facings and press the seam allowances towards the facings.

10. At the centre fronts, turn the facings to the right side of the garment along the cut-out section. Sew along the bottom edge, then bag out. Press the hems up to the finished length all the way around.

11. With right sides together, sew the front and back lining pieces together at the shoulders. Press the seams open. With right sides together, insert the sleeve linings into the lining body armholes, making sure you match the shoulder notches on the sleeves to the shoulder seams on the body. Sew the underarm and side seams in one continuous line of stitching on each side. Press the seams open.

12. To sew the pleat down across the top of the centre back neck of the lining, bring the two notches at the top of the centre back together to create a fold and pin in place.

13. With right sides together, pin and sew the lining body hem to the outer body hem. Press the seams into the lining. Pin the hem up in a few places so that it sits at its finished length.

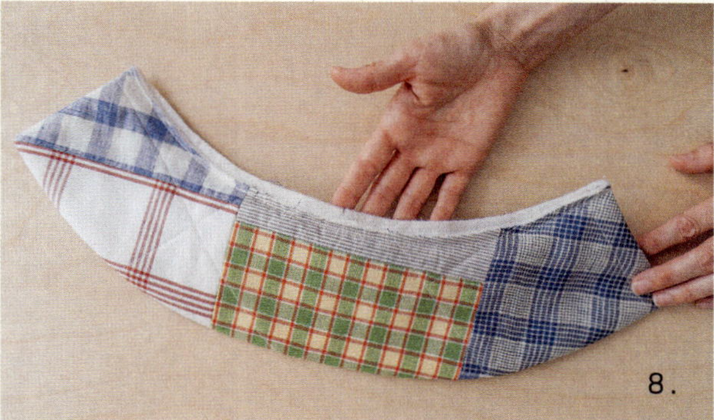
8.

10.

11.

12.

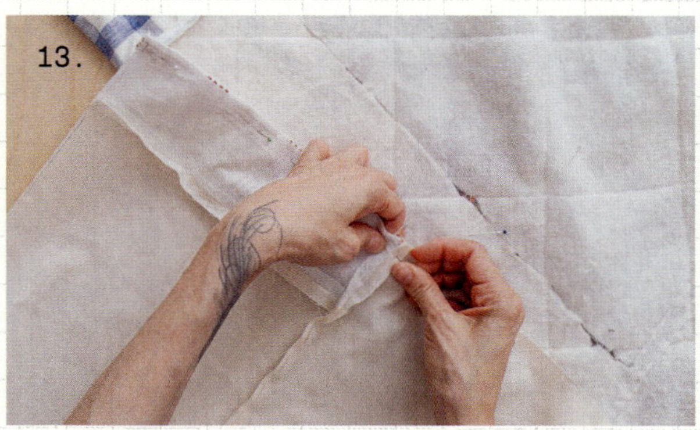
13.

14. Feed the lining sleeve inside your outer sleeve, wrong sides together, as if you are about to try on the coat.

15. Now turn the sleeve inside out. Fold the lining hem to the wrong side by 1 cm (⅜ in.) and pin the hems together, matching the underarm seams.

16. Now put your hand between the lining and outer sleeve (against the wrong sides), reach down to the sleeve hem and pull so that the outer and lining sleeves are inside out (photo 16a). With the original pin as a guide, you can now pin the hems in place right sides together, matching the underarm seams (photo 16b). Sew the hems, then pull your sleeves right side out.

17. Lift the body lining to the inside of the coat, wrong sides together. Place the lining under the facing, with the facing overlapping the lining by about 2 cm (¾ in.) all the way around. Pin the facing to the lining along the bound edges, making sure that the outside of the jacket also looks neat.

14.

15.

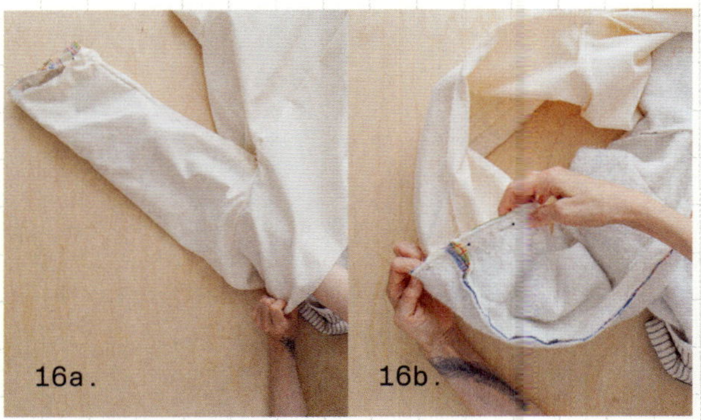
16a.
16b.

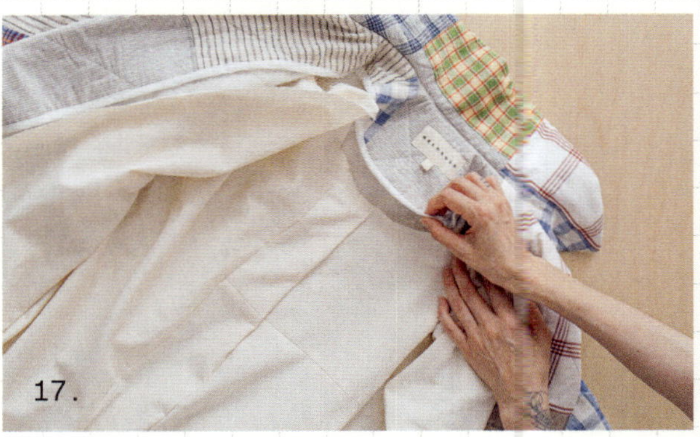
17.

18. Using running stitch, hand stitch the lining to the binding on the back neck facing, from shoulder point to shoulder point.

19. Now hand running stitch the front facings to the linings in the same way, without catching the outer coat or the pocket bags as you go. Once you get down towards the hems, there will be excess fabric in the lining length; fold up the excess lining neatly and place it under the sides of the front facings (it is shown pinned in place in the photo).

20. Pin and hand tack the hem in place close to the lining seam line, catching the outer coat slightly as you go around. Repeat the process with the sleeve hems.

21. To finish the coat, topstitch through all layers down the centre front edges and around the neckline (going under the collar) about 8 mm (¼ in.) away from the edges. This will hold the pieces together neatly and help the collar edges to roll out nicely.

22. Sew five buttons and horizontal buttonholes to the centre fronts (see page 30).

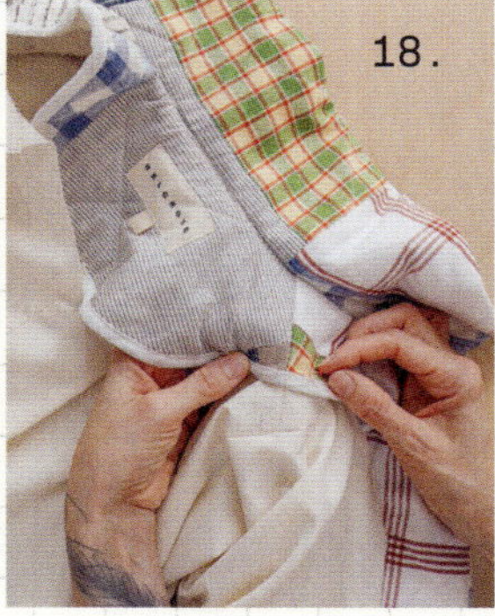
18.

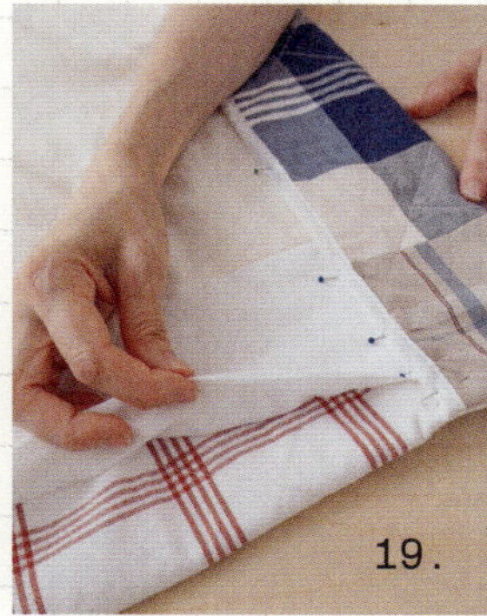
19.

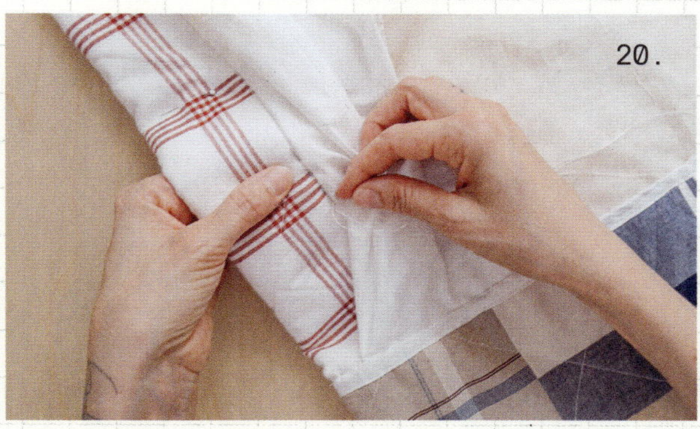
20.

21.

<u>Tip:</u> The first horizontal buttonhole on the coat front should be placed about 2.5 cm (1 in.) down from the top, with four more spaced about 15 cm (6 in.) apart below it.

EDITH WEARS THE QUILTED COAT IN A SIZE S/M, MADE USING TONE-ON-TONE LARGE SCRAPS FOR THE BODY AND SMALLER CONTRAST SCRAPS FOR THE COLLAR.

METHOD:

STRIPS

We came across this method when we first started using Birgitta's grandmother's loom and were collecting remnants to make into yarn balls for weaving rag rugs. We then continued to play around with the technique and develop other ways of using fabric yarn to create texture and decoration.

You can use this method in many ways, including adding straight lines onto a fabric base to create a surface pattern or using strips sewn closely together over a border of a garment to create lush and fluffy texture and weight.

This section provides a general overview, while the actual pattern of each surface texture used is shown in more detail in the individual projects. A tip to keep in mind is that this is a very organic type of process, so don't worry too much about it all being perfect – just play and have fun.

This method is particularly suited to projects that need some structure – for example, a short jacket or accessories such as bags. Even home furnishings such as cushion covers and upholstery all benefit from this technique.

STRIPS TOTE

RUFFLE SKIRT

SWIRL SHIRT

PLAID JACKET

CHOOSING FABRICS

Choose a mix of light-weight fabrics in any size of scraps and in any fibre type (although sometimes it is nice to keep the same fibres together). It can be a good idea to keep certain colours apart, particularly dark and light to avoid bleeding of colours if you wash anything later on. For example, you could join all dark, black and navy denim strips together, or multi-coloured and patterned fabrics, or white and light-coloured neutrals.

Here we will show you how to work with strips in two ways – straight strips (A) and bias strips (B).

OPTION A: STRAIGHT STRIPS

The strips can be cut from any fabric scraps in any direction you like and can be completely random. They are used as a way of adding texture and decoration to a base fabric. We usually cut our strips from small offcuts or selvedge edges – basically, any pieces that aren't easily usable in anything else. Over time we slowly save and put them together into yarn balls to be used at a later date. This application is very suited to home furnishings like textural cushion covers and accessories such as bags.

1.

1. Cut strips from scrap fabrics, making each strip approximately 2.5 cm (1 in.) wide (some variation is absolutely fine). You can cut the strips in any direction you like – straight grain, bias or any grain in between. Use a ruler to mark your lines if it helps, but you can also just estimate as this method doesn't have to be precise.

2.

2. Once you have cut a bunch of strips, you can sew them together using your machine. Overlap each strip by around 2.5–5 cm (1–2 in.) and then simply sew across through both layers to hold the strips together. We usually sew a diagonal line across, which is quite stable. Continue sewing all strips together in the same way.

3.

3. Once you're done, roll up the strips into a yarn ball. You can continue to add to the ball over time and build it up until you want to use it for a project.

   Now you can sew your strips onto a fabric base. In the next steps we will show you how to sew strips in even, straight lines, but you can get really creative and experiment with different patterns as you gain confidence.

4. Start by marking some straight lines on your base fabric, using a dissolvable fabric marker pen or tailor's chalk, in the direction you plan to sew your strips. These lines can be 5–10 cm (2–4 in.) apart, depending on how much guidance you want. See the individual project info for how far away from the edges you should begin sewing your strips.

5. Starting at one end of your fabric, sew on the first strip. Stitch through the very centre of the strip, sewing through all layers.

6. Continue adding strips side by side, leaving about 1 cm (⅜ in.) between each centre sewing line. Cut the strips to the required length from the yarn ball as you go.

7. Continue until you have covered the entire base piece with strips.

4.

5.

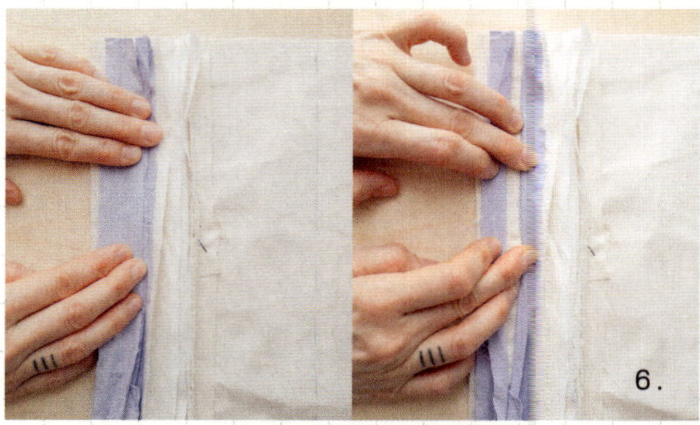
6.

7.

OPTION B: BIAS (GATHERED) STRIPS

Note: For this technique, you will need a gathering foot for your machine.

This application is very suited to use on garments, as the edges don't fray in the way they do when working with option A. Cutting this way means that the raw edges simply become soft and fluffy, so the project can handle wash and wear over time.

These strips are cut on the bias of the fabric, in a similar way to how binding is cut. When using bias strips, it is usually easier to cut what you need when you are actually working on your project, rather than making yarn balls.

For the projects in this book, we also gathered the strips through the centre to add more texture, so this is how we will show you this method below – but you can use flat strips if you prefer. As with option A, this is a way of adding texture and decoration to a base fabric.

1. Choose a selection of scraps you would like to use. We recommend cutting strips from 3–4 layers of fabrics at the same time. The example here shows how to fold your fabric to cut longer strips on the bias (this works well for a slightly larger piece of fabric).

2. Start by establishing the diagonal bias line of your fabric as best you can, looking at the existing weave/grainline, and cut along this line. Fold the fabric up along the bias line.

3. Make a couple more folds along the same line.

4. Mark your strips using a ruler (the individual projects will specify what widths you should work with). Here we are cutting strips that are 4 cm (1½ in.) wide, so make marks 4 cm (1½ in.) apart across the top and bottom of your folded piece and then draw the lines in using your ruler and a dissolvable fabric marker pen or tailor's chalk. Depending on the project, you may want to use several different widths of strip.

2.

3.

4.

5. Cut along the drawn lines to separate the fabric into strips.

6. Now you can gather all of your strips together, making one long length. Start by attaching a gathering foot to your machine; do a quick sample first to see how it works for your machine. The longer the stitch length, the more gathers there will be. Once you are happy with your sample gather amount, start sewing through the centre of each strip so that it gathers as you go.

7. When you get towards the end of each strip, underlap the next strip by around 2.5 cm (1 in.) and continue sewing. This will give you one long gathered strip that joins as you go.

8. Continue adding strips in this way until you have the length you need.

9. Now you can sew your gathered strips onto your base fabric in the same way as for Option A, onto a base fabric and through the middle of the strip (see page 110).

5.

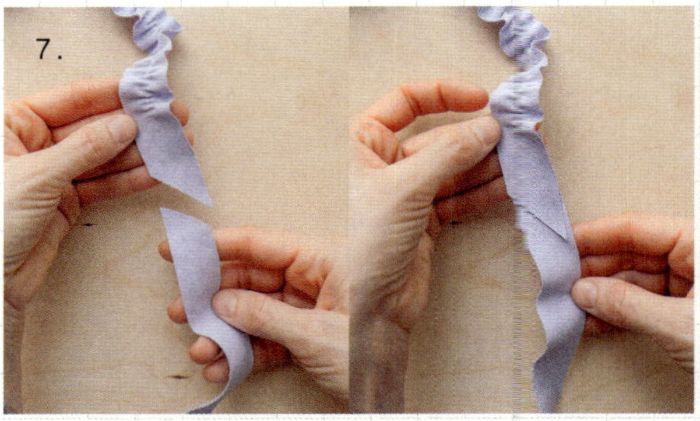
7.

Note: Why specifically underlap? Well, this is because it will make the process of sewing much smoother. When you put the new fabric underneath the one you are currently sewing, it stops the new fabric from being dragged by the foot and bunching up.

8.

STRIP VARIATIONS

Here is a selection of ideas using the strips method, showing different patterns and colours, to help inspire your projects.

OPTION 1:

Straight strips 2.5 cm (1 in.) wide, sewn in vertical lines 1 cm (⅜ in.) apart; cream tone on tone.

OPTION 2:

Straight strips 2.5 cm (1 in.) wide, sewn in vertical lines 1 cm (⅜ in.) apart; multi-coloured strips.

OPTION 3:

Bias gathered strips, 2 cm (¾ in.) wide, sewn in a swirl pattern; white.

OPTION 4:

Bias gathered strips, 2 cm (¾ in.) wide, sewn in a swirl pattern; black.

OPTION 5:

Bias gathered strips, 2.5 cm, 3 cm and 3.5 cm (1, 1¼ and 1⅜ in.) wide, sewn in a geometric plaid arrangement; multi-coloured strips.

OPTION 6:

Bias gathered strips, 2.5 cm, 3 cm and 3.5 cm (1, 1¼ and 1⅜ in.) wide, sewn in a geometric plaid arrangement; neutral tones.

OPTION 7:

Bias gathered strips, 4 cm (1½ in.) wide, sewn 1 cm (⅜ in.) apart in a swirl arrangement; tone on tone.

OPTION 8:

Bias gathered strips, 4 cm (1½ in.) wide, sewn 1 cm (⅜ in.) apart in a swirl arrangement; multi-coloured strips.

1.

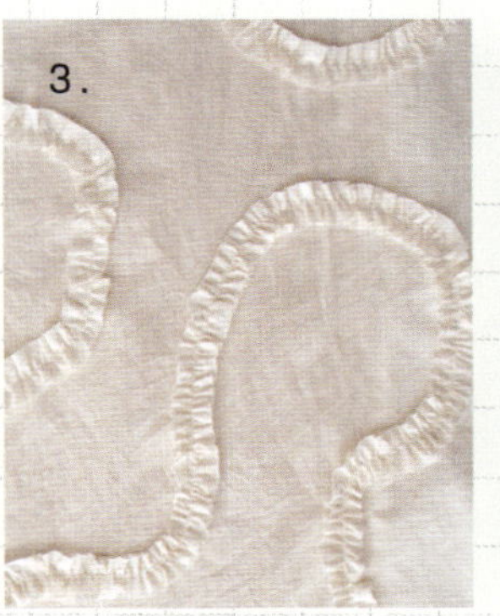

3.

5.

8.

STRIPS TOTE

After doing a run of Helgrose garments a few years ago, we decided to plan a project that would use up the scraps right from the start and landed on the idea of making neutral and denim tote bags. Since then, we have displayed various versions in our shop window and it has become a constant talking point for people walking by, who then pop in to check out what we do. It truly defines the ethos of Helgrose and the zero-waste production model in a visual way. Even though there are a lot of loose threads and fraying with this method, applied in the right way it adds a beautiful texture that ages well. Embrace the fray – it's part of its beauty!

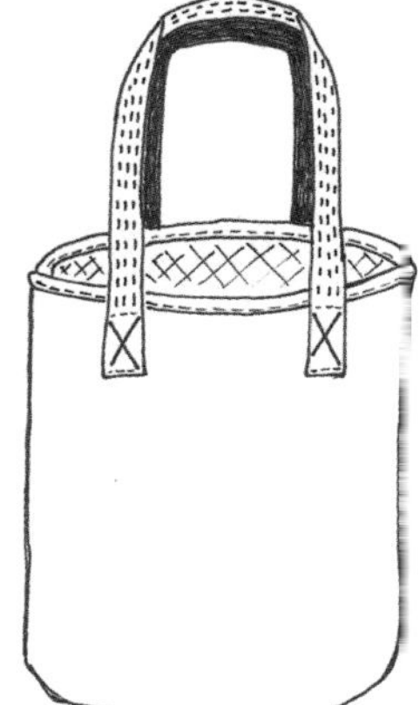

SKILL LEVEL ●●○○○

TECHNIQUES

Straight strips

SIZE MADE

Finished tote is 48 cm (19 in.) wide by 50 cm (20 in.) long.

PATTERN

There's no pattern – just cut the pieces following the instructions below. You can adjust the size of this tote however you like and use the same method.

FABRIC

Medium- to heavy-weight cotton for the base fabric. Light- to medium-weight cotton and linen remnants for the strips.

NOTIONS

300 cm (118 in.) binding, 4 cm (1½ in.) wide, to finish the seams.

METHOD

CUTTING & PREPARATION

Note: If you are patchworking the bag base and straps, sew the seams with a 1-cm (⅜-in.) seam allowance, right sides together, and press the seams open. Topstitch each side of the seams to secure the seam allowances, sewing about 8 mm (¼ in.) away from the seamline; this will ensure that the seams sit flat when you sew on your decorative strips.

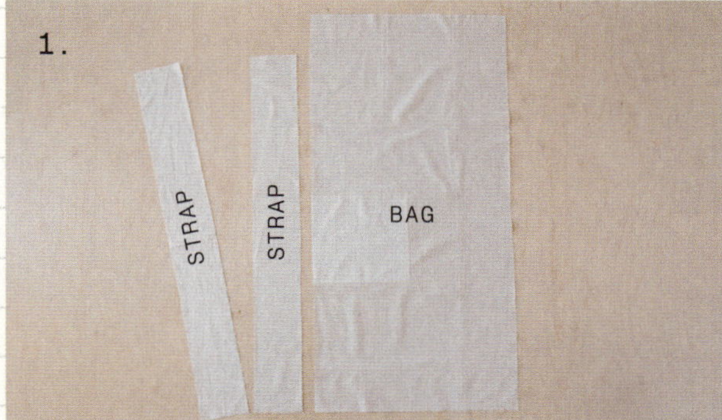

1. Cut out all your tote bag pattern pieces following the measurements given below. You can either use fabric cut from the roll or, as we have done, patchwork together the base bag piece and straps using fabric offcuts.

   The final base pieces should measure:
   Bag x 1: 50 x 100 cm (20 x 40 in.)
   Straps x 2: 12 x 80 cm (4¾ x 31½ in.)

2. Prepare yarn balls of straight strips to use for the bag (see page 109).

Note: The seam allowances for the side seams of the bag construction are 1.5 cm (⅝ in.).

SEWING

1. Sew the strips vertically onto the bag base piece, on the wrong side of the fabric, starting 2.5 cm (1 in.) in from each long edge. Sew the centre stitch lines of the strips approximately 1 cm (⅜ in.) apart (see page 110).

2. Attach binding (see page 37) to the long vertical edges (these will be your side seams). Then attach binding across the short edges, top and bottom, leaving an extra tail of binding on each end of around 2.5 cm (1 in.).

3. Fold the bag in half, right sides together, matching up the short edges, and sew the side seams, making sure you keep the first strips that you sewed along the edges out of the way.

4. At the bottom of one side, fold the bag so that the side seam sits directly on top of the bottom edge, creating a triangular shape with the side seam running through the centre, as shown here. Sew a line across; your finished stitch line should measure 10 cm (4 in.) across. Repeat on the other side of the bag.

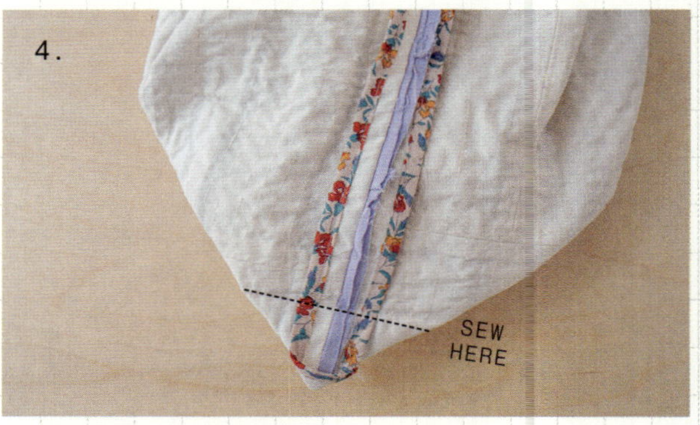

Tip: Take care sewing step 4: this part can be quite bulky, as you're sewing through all layers, including the strips and bound edges.

5. Take one of your strap pieces and press 1 cm (⅜ in.) to the wrong side along all edges.

6. Fold the entire strap piece in half, wrong sides together, to make a long narrow strip and pin.

7. Topstitch the strap together all around, close to the edges, making sure you join the open ends together on both layers. Add three more rows of topstitching through the centre of the straps, spacing them evenly. Repeat steps 5–7 to make the second strap.

8. There are binding tails at the top of the side seams (photo 8a). Neatly tuck them in and hand tack in place (photo 8b).

9. Turn the bag right side out. On the front of the bag, place a strap end 10 cm (4 in.) in from the side seams and extending 9 cm (3½ in.) below the top edge. Pin in place, making sure the strap is not twisted. Repeat on the back of the bag.

10. Topstitch the straps to the bag in a rectangular shape, stitching a cross through the middle, and working through all layers.

5.

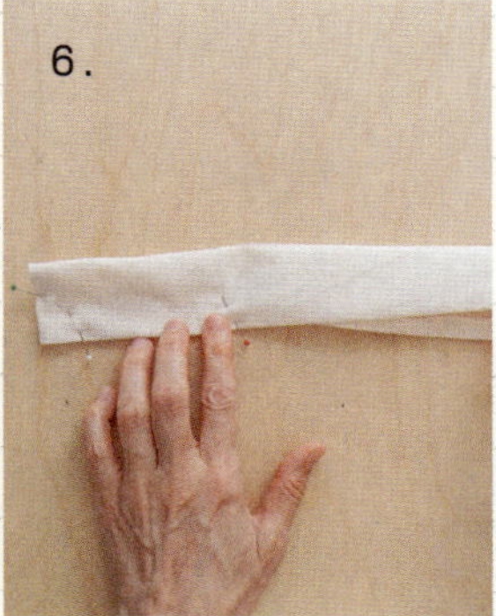
6.

7.

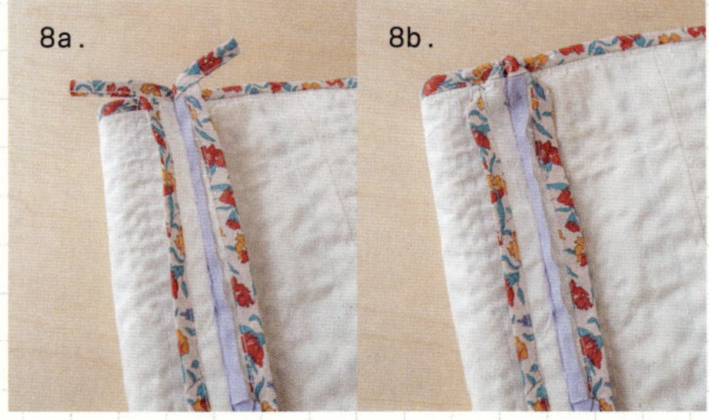
8a. 8b.

9.

10.

RUFFLE SKIRT

This skirt was originally made for the Birgitta Helmersson label, in both a multi-coloured and a black version. People were immediately drawn to the texture and movement created by the ruffles. We used a wavelike pattern, but you can play around with different shapes and patterns. The more strips you add, the more weight will be added to the garment – so keep this in mind when you are planning your project. As these strips are cut on the bias, the edges will not fray but will become soft and fluffy with wash and wear.

SKILL LEVEL 

TECHNIQUES

Bias gathered strips

SIZE MADE

4XL (cream and multi-colour) worn by Sarah,
M (black) worn by Anna

PATTERN

There's no pattern – just cut the pieces following the size chart in the Cutting section on page 124. (Refer to the Comfort Pants waist and hip sizing in How to Use This Book, page 19, to choose the right size for you.)

FABRIC

For this project, we patchworked together the pieces for the skirt using larger fabric offcuts and overlocked the seams together (see page 52). We used similar colours in light-weight organic cottons. For the ruffles, we used various offcuts in different sizes and colours.

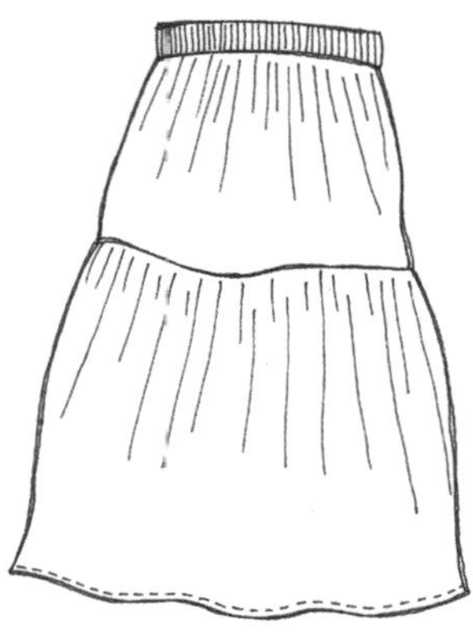

NOTIONS

	XS	S	M	L	XL	2XL	3XL	4XL	5XL	6XL
BIAS BINDING: 4 CM (1½ IN.) WIDE, IN A LIGHT-WEIGHT COTTON TO FINISH THE INSIDE OF THE WAISTBAND	110 cm (43½ in.)	115 cm (45½ in.)	120 cm (47½ in.)	125 cm (49½ in.)	130 cm (51½ in.)	135 cm (53½ in.)	140 cm (55½ in.)	145 cm (57 in.)	150 cm (59 in.)	155 cm (61 in.)
ELASTIC: 3 CM (1¼ IN.) WIDE	70 cm (27½ in.)	75 cm (29½ in.)	80 cm (3½ in.)	85 cm (33½ in.)	90 cm (35½ in.)	95 cm (37½ in.)	100 cm (39½ in.)	105 cm (41½ in.)	110 cm (43½ in.)	115 cm (45½ in.)

ANNA WEARS A RUFFLE SKIRT IN A SIZE M, MADE USING BLACK TONE-ON-TONE RUFFLES.

METHOD

CUTTING

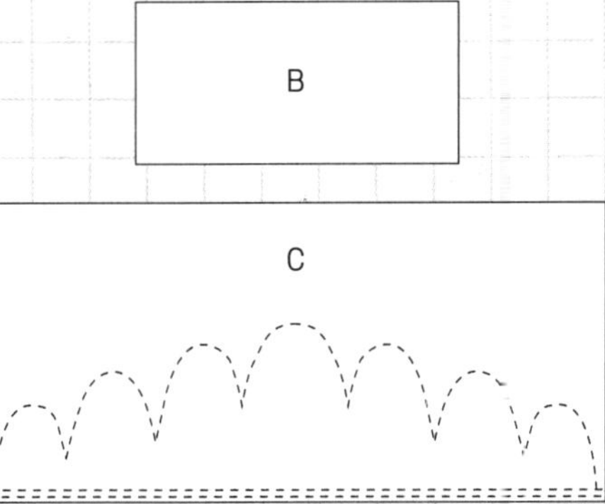

1. Cut out all your skirt pieces for your chosen size, referring to the chart below.

2. Referring to the diagram for a rough layout of the shapes, mark out your border lines on the skirt hem with a piece of tailor's chalk or a dissolvable fabric marker pen; the hem turn-up – 1 + 1 cm (⅜ + ⅜ in.) – is also shown in this diagram. We created a wavelike pattern across the bottom; the middle wave has a height of approximately 33 cm (13 in.), slowly getting a little smaller towards the side seams, and the final one near the side seam has a height of approximately 18 cm (7 in.).

	XS	S	M	L	XL	2XL	3XL	4XL	5XL	6XL
WAISTBAND (A): CUT 2 (WIDTH X LENGTH)	55 x 9 cm (21½ x 3½ in.)	57.5 x 9 cm (22½ x 3½ in.)	60 x 9 cm (23½ x 3½ in.)	62.5 x 9 cm (24½ x 3½ in.)	65 x 9 cm (25½ x 3½ in.)	67.5 x 9 cm (26½ x 3½ in.)	70 x 9 cm (27½ x 3½ in.)	72.5 x 9 cm (28½ x 3½ in.)	75 x 9 cm (29½ x 3½ in.)	77.5 x 9 cm (30½ x 3½ in.)
TOP TIER (B): CUT 2 (WIDTH X LENGTH)	55 x 28 cm (21½ x 11 in.)	57.5 x 29 cm (22½ x 11½ in.)	60 x 30 cm (23½ x 12 in.)	62.5 x 31 cm (24½ x 12¼ in.)	65 x 32 cm (25½ x 12½ in.)	67.5 x 33 cm (26½ x 13 in.)	70 x 34 cm (27½ x 13½ in.)	72.5 x 35 cm (28½ x 13¾ in.)	75 x 36 cm (29½ x 14 in.)	77.5 x 37 cm (30½ x 14½ in.)
BOTTOM TIER (C): CUT 2 (WIDTH X LENGTH)	105 x 53 cm (41½ x 21 in.)	110 x 54 cm (43½ x 21¼ in.)	115 x 55 cm (45¼ x 21½ in.)	120 x 56 cm (47¼ x 22 in.)	125 x 57 cm (49¼ x 22½ in.)	130 x 58 cm (51¼ x 23 in.)	135 x 59 cm (53¼ x 23¼ in.)	140 x 60 cm (55 x 23½ in.)	145 x 61 cm (57 x 24 in.)	150 x 62 cm (59 x 24½ in.)

BIAS GATHERED STRIPS

Cut bias strips approximately 4 cm (1½ in.) wide from the scrap fabrics you have chosen and sew them together to the length you require (see pages 112–113). The amount of gathered bias strips varies depending on the skirt size you are using and how many ruffles you want to use, but you can build up the amount you need as you go. If you are filling a relatively large size along the bottom, as in this project, then you will need a decent amount of fabric. This is a great scrap-busting project, as you can get through quite a lot of remnants to create the ruffles.

BIAS GATHERED STRIPS

Note: All seam allowances are 1 cm (⅜ in.) unless otherwise stated.

2. SEWING

SEWING

3.

1. Press the hems up on the front and back bottom tiers of the skirt to the wrong side by 1 cm (⅜ in.) and then again by 1 cm (⅜ in.). Topstitch the hems close to the fold line.

2. Sew one row of ruffles along the hems of the front and back bottom tiers, starting and finishing about 2 cm (¾ in.) from the side seams and leaving a 'tail' of ruffle about 5 cm (2 in.) long on one side. The centre of the ruffle should sit on the hem turn-up, so that the ruffle extends a little way past the finished skirt length.

3. Sew on a length of ruffles along the upper outline of the border design on the front and back bottom tiers (the wave border lines that you drew in on step 2 of the Cutting section). The centre stitch line of the waves should be about 2 cm (¾ in.) away from the raw side edges.

4. Sew two more rows of ruffles – one above the row on the hem and one below the first row of 'waves'. The centre of each row should be about 2 cm (¾ in.) from the centre of the adjoining row.

5. Now fill in each of the 'waves' one at a time, working your way from the outer edges and continuing around and around in a circular motion until the whole area has been covered.

6. Place the front and back bottom tiers right sides together and sew the side seams, making sure you neatly line up the hems and keep the ruffles out of the way along the bottom. Overlock the seam allowances together, leaving a small tail of overlocking at the bottom. Tuck this tail inside the seam and secure it with a few small stitches. Press the seams towards the back. Topstitch to hold the seam allowances in place.

7. Sew the excess length of ruffle from step 2 across the seam, overlapping over the ruffles on the other side, to cover the side seam and make the ruffles look seamless.

8. Place the front and back top tier pieces right sides together and sew the side seams. Overlock the seam allowances together and press towards the back.

9. Place the front and back waistband pieces right sides together and sew one side seam. Press the seam open.

4.

6.

7.

10. Bind one long edge of the waistband (see page 42).

11. Sew the other side seam of the waistband. Press the seam open.

12. Gather the top edge of the bottom tier by working two rows of stitching close together, around 6 mm (¼ in.) away from the edge, leaving loose tails of thread on each end. Pull the bobbin threads to gather in the edge to fit the bottom edge of the top tier. Tie the threads securely together on each end and even out the gathers.

13. With right sides together, sew the front/back bottom tier to the front/back top tier, matching the side seams as you go. Overlock the seam allowances together and press the seam allowance up into the top tier.

14. Attach the waistband to the top tier of the skirt, making sure you match the side seams, and insert the elastic (see pages 42–43).

14.

SWIRL SHIRT

This project is based on an idea we had of doing a zero-waste garment using a 'conventional' pattern. We cut all the offcuts into bias strips and then gathered them together and added them onto the shirt in a swirl-like pattern as a textural surface decoration. For the base, we used a large piece of cotton shirting left over from a previous job. This is one of our favourite projects, as it turns a classic bowler shirt into something extra special while remaining super wearable.

SKILL LEVEL ●●●○○

TECHNIQUES

Bias gathered strips

SIZE MADE

Size M/L, worn by Anti

FABRIC

Light-weight cotton voile, 135–145 cm (53–57 in.) wide. (You can use a narrower width than this, but you will need to allow for more fabric and re-arrange the layout plan according to the width and size you are using.) The amount of fabric you need varies depending on the pattern size you are making; see the layout plans on page 132 for an estimate on how much fabric you need based on your size. Depending on how much decoration you are adding to your shirt, you may need a little more of the main fabric for bias strips. You can either account for this in the estimate of the total fabric usage (so around 20–30 cm/8–12 in. more, shown in the layout plans) or preferably add in what you need using similar-coloured remnants from your scrap box.

NOTIONS

- Five buttons, each 15 mm (⅝ in.) wide.
- Light-weight iron-on interfacing for the front facing, back facing and half the collar piece. You will need approximately 40 x 85 cm (16 x 34 in.).

PATTERN

The Swirl Shirt is made using the Workwear Jacket pattern. The pattern pieces and adjustments required are outlined here:

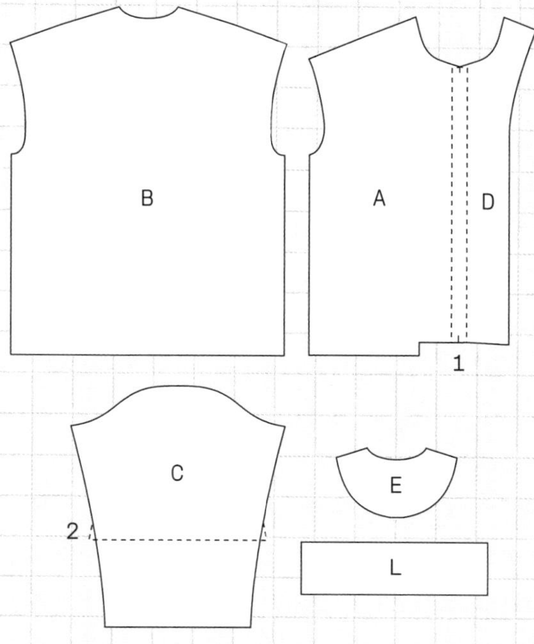

Pattern pieces

- A: Front body
- B: Back body
- C: Workwear sleeve
- D: Front facing
- E: Back facing
- L: Bowler collar

Pattern adjustments

1. Overlap the front body (A) and the front facing (D) by 4 cm (1½ in.) along the long centre front edges and stick them together to make one pattern piece (a grown-on facing). Mark a centre front notch top and bottom at the exact centre point of the two overlapped pieces – see the diagram.
2. Use the short sleeve cutting line on the main Workwear Jacket sleeve pattern.

LAYOUT PLANS

This project is made using fabric off the roll, with all the offcuts cut into bias strips that will be attached as a detail to the shirt. Alternatively, you could cut the shirt from several larger leftover pieces of a similar colour and weight of fabric.

These diagrams show the pattern pieces required and a guide to how to lay out your pattern pieces when cutting. Follow the layout plan for the size you are working with. The layouts account for an extra 20–30 cm (8–12 in.), which you will need to cut the bias strips. Alternatively, you can use other leftover fabrics of a similar weight and colour. Keep in mind that these layouts are based on a fabric width of 135–145 cm (53–57 in.), so the placement of your pattern pieces may vary slightly depending on the size you are making and the fabric width you are using.

Cut – main fabric: all sizes

- A/D: Front body/front facing – 1 pair
- B: Back body - 1
- C: Workwear sleeve – 1 pair
- E: Back facing - 1
- L: Bowler collar - 1

Interfacing: all sizes

Apply interfacing to the front facings (D) up to the centre front notch points, and half the collar lengthways (L), as shown with light grey shading in the diagrams.

Layout plan: sizes XS/S–L/XL

You will need a piece of fabric approximately 135–145 cm (53–57 in.) wide by 190 cm (75 in.) long.

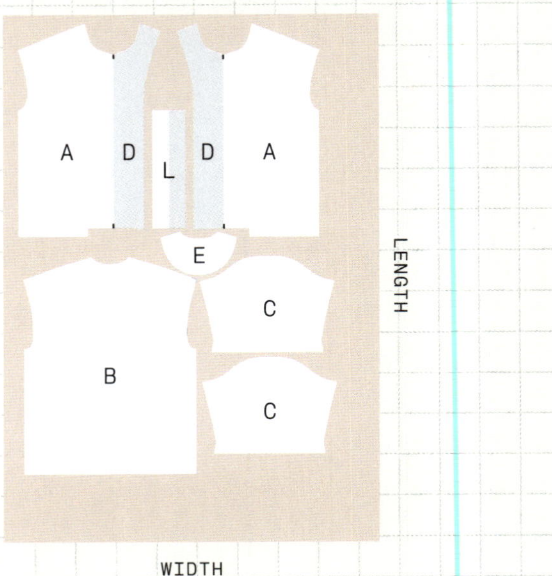

Layout plan: sizes XL/2XL–5XL/6XL

You will need a piece of fabric approximately 135–145 cm (53–57 in.) wide by 250 cm (98 in.) long.

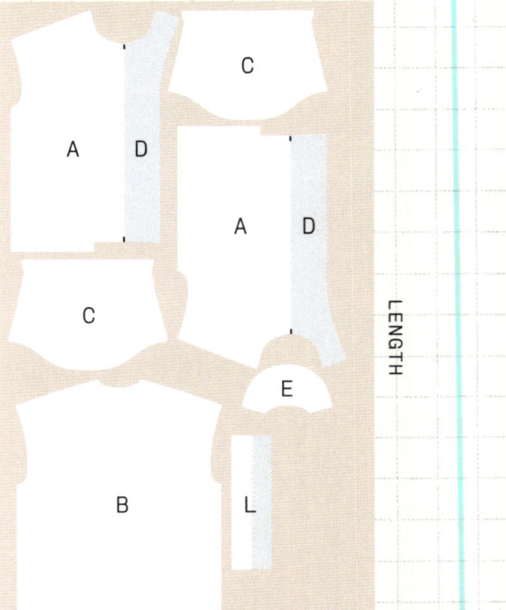

METHOD

BIAS GATHERED STRIPS

The ruffles for this shirt are made using all the fabric left over after cutting the garment out (essentially, all the negative space between the pattern pieces).

1. Determine the bias angle of each piece, based on the original grainlines, then mark and cut bias strips approximately 2 cm (¾ in.) wide.

2. Stitch the strips together, gathering them at the same time by stitching through the centre, using a gathering foot on your sewing machine (see steps 6–8 on page 112).

Note: All seam allowances are 1 cm (⅜ in.) unless otherwise stated.

SEWING

1. Sew the side seams of your front and back body pieces, right sides together. Overlock the seam allowances together and press towards the back.

2. On the right side of the fabric, place your ruffles in a swirly pattern across the front and back body pieces, collar and sleeves (photo 2a). Pin, then topstitch in place, sewing through the centre of the ruffles as you go (photo 2b).

3. With right sides together, sew the shoulder seams of the front and back body pieces. Overlock the seam allowances together and press towards the back. Sew the shoulder seams of the grown-on front facings and the separate back facing, right sides together, then press the seams open.

1. BIAS GATHERED STRIPS

2a. SEWING

2b.

4. Overlock the raw edges of the facing pieces, then press to the wrong side by approximately 8 mm (¼ in.) all the way around. Topstitch in place.

5. Fold the sleeves in half, right sides together, then sew the underarm seams. Overlock the seam allowances together and press towards the back.

6. With right sides together, insert the sleeve heads into the armholes, making sure you match the shoulder notch on the sleeves to the shoulder seams on the body and match the underam seams of the sleeves to the side seams of the body. Sew in place, overlock the seam allowances together and press the seam allowances down into the sleeves.

7. Press the sleeve hems to the wrong side by 1 cm (⅜ in.), then press up a second time as far as the notch. Pin in place and topstitch close to the fold.

8. Fold the collar in half widthways, right sides together, and stitch the short sides.

9. Turn the collar right side out and press neatly. Machine stitch across the long raw edge to hold the two layers together, about 8 mm (¼ in.) away from the raw edges.

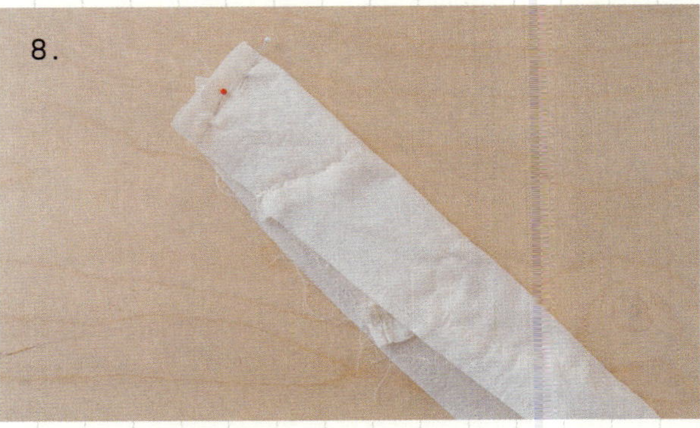

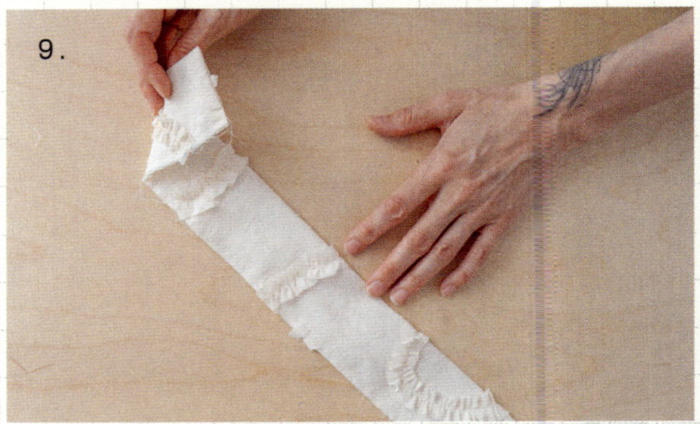

10. Attach the collar to the neck: line up the centre back notch on the collar with the centre back neck and line up the outer edges of the collar with the notches on the front necks that indicate the collar start point. (The construction is very similar to attaching the Workwear Jacket collar, so refer to page 39.)

11. Fold back the front facing at the centre front notch point, right sides together, and pin the facing neck to the front body neck, matching the shoulder seams and sandwiching the collar in between the two layers. Sew together with a 1-cm (⅜-in.) seam allowance, then turn right side out and press the facing and collar neatly in place.

12. Press the hem to the wrong side by 1 cm (⅜ in.) all the way around (just not at the cut-out section at the centre fronts). With right sides together, fold the facings back at the centre front notch point along the cut-out section at the hem. Sew along the bottom edge, then turn the front cut-out section right side out and press neatly in place. Topstitch the hems and facings down all the way around (see page 41).

13. Press the collar/front facing back to a nice 'break point', then add buttons and vertical buttonholes down the centre front (see page 30). Your first button should start just below the break point and the remaining four should be spaced about 10 cm (4 in.) apart.

13.

PLAID JACKET

At the beginning of 2024 we were testing out new ideas and made some garments with a method we called 'stitched plaid', where lines of contrasting thread were sewn onto fabric to create the look of a check or plaid-type pattern (you can see this in the pants worn with the Workwear Jacket project in the photo on page 85). We then took the concept one step further by using gathered bias strips in different layers and we absolutely loved the outcome! This version is quite colourful, but it also looks amazing with tone-on-tone fabrics as it creates a beautiful texture on the surface of the jacket.

SKILL LEVEL ●●●●○

TECHNIQUES

Bias gathered strips

SIZE MADE

S/M worn by Ludjero

FABRIC

Light- to medium-weight cotton for the base fabric of the jacket. We patchworked together a couple of larger pieces of repurposed and vintage fabrics in a pale check pattern. We find that using a base fabric that already has checks or stripes on it can help with the placement of the gathered strips, as well as adding to the overall plaid effect. However, you could use fabric off the roll for this – see page 12 for more on fabric usage by size.

NOTIONS

- 200 cm (80 in.) binding, 4 cm (1½ in.) wide, in light-weight cotton.*
- Approximately 75 x 120 cm (30 x 48 in.) medium-weight woven iron-on interfacing for the front facings, back facing, one collar and the body and sleeve hems, as shown in the layout plans.*
- Four buttons, each 20mm (¾ in.).

* This is a general estimate and applies to all garment sizes, so you may have a little left over.

PATTERN

The Plaid Jacket is made using the Workwear Jacket pattern. The only changes are that you use the coat sleeve (P) and follow the coat underarm line on the front and back bodies (A and B). All the pattern pieces required are shown in the Layout Plans.

LAYOUT PLANS

This project is cut from fabric that we patchworked together using large offcuts in different striped and checked fabrics. The sizes required have been organized into three separate layout plans (1, 2 and 3) to ensure you get the most efficient layout. (Alternatively you can cut using fabric off the roll; if so, follow the Workwear Jacket pattern, page 12, for fabric estimates by size, as the usage is similar.)

- A: Front body* – 1 pair
- B: Back body* – 1
- D: Front facing - 1 pair
- E: Back facing - 1
- F: Workwear collar – 1 pair
- I: Chest pocket - 1
- J: Hip pocket – 1 pair
- P: Coat sleeve – 1 pair

* Make sure you follow the Coat sleeve underarm line on the pattern.

Patchwork fabric

Layout plan 1

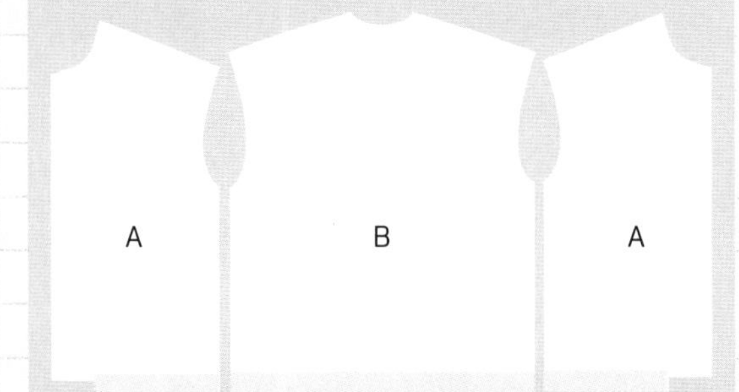

Layout plan 2

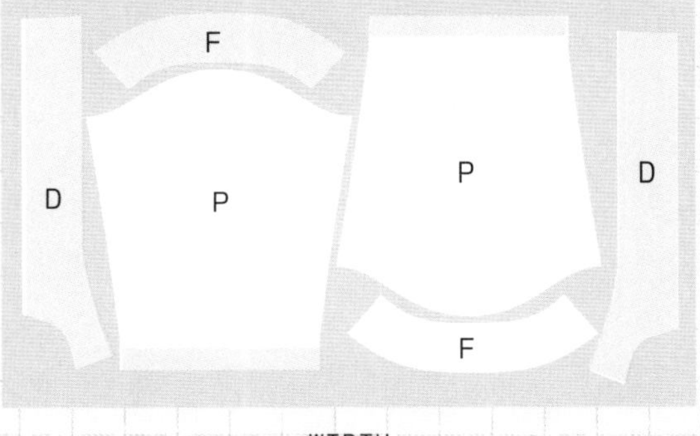

Layout plan 3

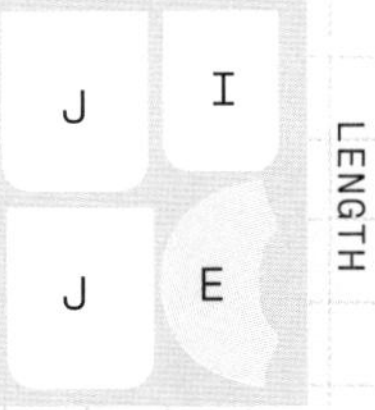

METHOD

PATCHWORK, CUTTING & INTERFACING

1. Patchwork together three different fabric sizes. To do this, start by laying out the required pattern pieces in your size, as shown in layout plans 1, 2 and 3. Measure the width and length for the total amount of fabric you need for each, allowing 2.5 cm (1 in.) extra all around.

2. Lay out and sew together your patchwork to the sizes required. You will need to overlap all of your patchwork pieces by 2 cm (¾ in.), to allow for a seam allowance of 1 cm (⅜ in.). Sew the seams using the Stitch and Overlock method (see page 52): overlock the seam allowances together, press to one side, then topstitch all seam allowances down around 8 mm (¼ in.) away from the seam.

3. Pin the paper patterns to the patchwork fabric following layout plans 1, 2 and 3 and cut out all your pieces.

4. Apply medium-weight iron on interfacing to the wrong side of one collar piece (F), the front facings (D), the back facing (E), and a strip 5 cm (2 in.) wide along the body and sleeve hems, as shown by the grey shaded areas on layout plans 1, 2 and 3.

2.

> Note: You will need to use a gathering foot on your machine for this.

BIAS GATHERED STRIPS

Choose three different fabric types to use for the bias gathered strips. The amount you need will vary depending on which garment size you are making, but as a rough guide you will need to prepare the following finished lengths:

- Ruffle 1 (double horizontal line): 2.5 cm (1 in.) wide by 11.5 m (12½ yd) long
- Ruffle 2 (double vertical line): 3 cm (1¼ in.) wide by 10 m (11 yd) long
- Ruffle 3 (single horizontal line): 3.5 cm (1⅜ in.) wide by 9.5 m (10⅜ yd) long

Stitch your ruffle pieces together, gathering them at the same time by stitching through the centre, using a gathering foot on your sewing machine (see page 112).

The placements we have given are based on the checked fabric we used as the main fabric. If you are using a different type of stripe or check, or a plain fabric, arrange your ruffles where they look best, so please consider this as just a guide.

Note: All seam allowances are 1 cm (⅜ in.) unless otherwise stated.

SEWING

1. Place the front and back body pieces right sides together and sew the side seams. Overlock the seam allowances together and press towards the back.

2. With right sides together, sew the front facings to the front body pieces along the long straight edge. Press the seams towards the facings. Understitch the facings close to the seam line, through the facing and seam allowances only (see page 28).

3. Using a piece of chalk or a dissolvable fabric marker pen, mark a dashed horizontal line 20 cm (8 in.) up from the hem to show where the first line of ruffle 1 should be placed. (This is measured up from the longest part of the hem, not the part where there is a cut-out at the front hems.)

   Mark a second horizontal line 4 cm (1½ in.) above the first one. Continue to mark double sets of lines 11 cm (4 ⅜ in.) and 4 cm (1½ in.) apart, as far up the body as you can go. You should end up with three or four sets of double lines, depending on which garment size you have cut out.

4. Pin the centre of the ruffles in place along the lines, cutting the strips to size where required when you get up to the armholes. Stitch the ruffles in place, stitching along the centre gather line.

3.

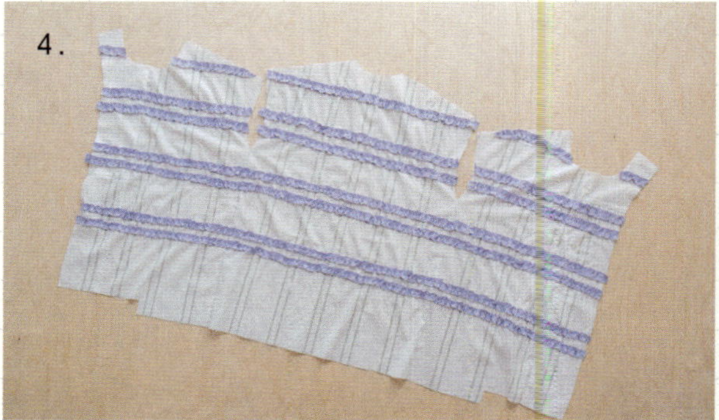
4.

Tip: If the final set of double ruffles is quite close to the top of the shoulders, then you only need to do one row. This will make it less bulky and easier to sew together around the shoulders and collar.

5. Mark a double row of dashed vertical lines to show where ruffle 2 should be placed. Start by establishing your centre back point, then mark a set of lines 3.5 cm (1⅜ in.) away from the centre back on each side (so these first lines will be a total of 7 cm/2¾ in. apart). Mark your second lines 3 cm (1¼ in.) away from your first lines. Now continue around the body on each side, marking sets of lines 7 cm (2¾ in.) and 3 cm (1¼ in.) apart until you get close to the front facings. Do not continue the ruffles onto the facing sections, and make sure that the last strip is at least 4 cm (1½ in.) away from the facing seam to allow for where the buttons and buttonholes will be placed at a later stage.

   Pin the centre of the ruffles in place along the lines and stitch the ruffles in place, stitching along the centre gather line.

6. Mark a single row of horizontal lines to show where ruffle 3 should be, the first one starting below the first double ruffle, and spacing them all evenly between the double sets of ruffle 1. Pin and sew in place.

7. Work out where you want the ruffles to go on the sleeves, pocket pieces and one of the collar pieces and stitch them in place. Keep in mind that the tops of the pockets will be folded down as far as the notch. Place them in a similar way to the body. The pockets and collar will not need as many ruffles, but you can place a small amount of each where it looks good to the eye.

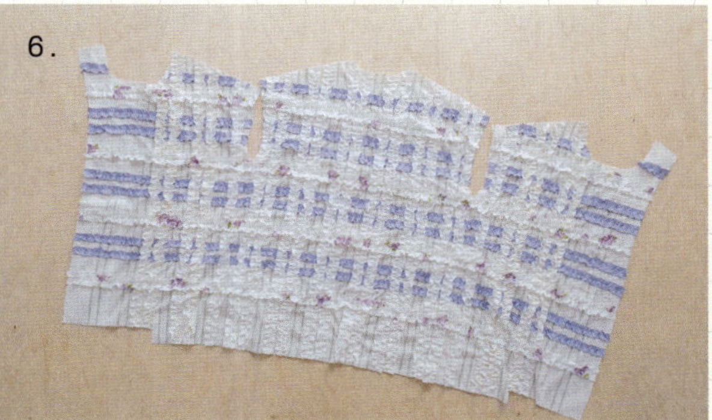

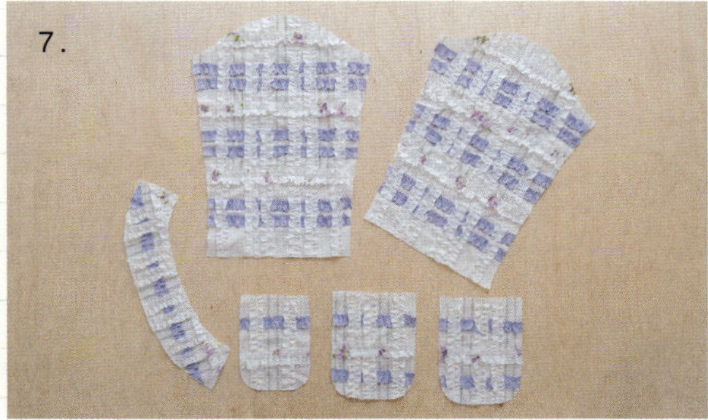

8. Topstitch around all edges of the pieces that have ruffles, about 8 mm (¼ in.) away from the raw edges, to hold the ruffles down neatly before you sew the rest of the garment together.

9. With right sides together, sew the front and back pieces together at the shoulder seams. Overlock the seam allowances together and press towards the back.

10. With right sides together, sew the underarm seams of the sleeves. Overlock the seam allowances together and press towards the back.

11. With right sides together, insert the sleeve heads into the armholes, making sure you match the shoulder notch on the sleeves to the shoulder seams on the body and match the underarm seams of the sleeves to the side seams of the body. Sew in place, overlock the seam allowances together and press the seam allowances down into the sleeves.

12. Press the sleeve hems up to the wrong side by 1 cm (⅜ in.), then press up a second time as far as the notch. Pin and then hand stitch in place so that the stitching is not visible from the right side.

13. With right sides together, sew the shoulder seams of the front and back facing pieces. Press the seams open.

14. Bind the outer edge of the facing, starting at one hem end and finishing at the other (see page 37).

15. Sew the collar together and then attach it to the neck of the jacket (see page 39) you do not need to topstitch around the collar for this version – just secure the raw edges together before attaching it to the neck. With right sides together, pin the facing around the neck of the body, sandwiching the collar in between. Stitch in place, then stitch along the centre front edges to attach the facings to the body of the jacket all the way down (see pages 39–41). Open out the facings and press the seam allowances towards the facings.

16. Press the hem to the wrong side by 1 cm (⅜ in.) all the way around, except for the cut-out section at the centre fronts). With right sides together, fold the facings back at the seam point along the cut-out section at the hem. Sew along the bottom edge, then turn the front cut-out section right side out and press neatly in place. Press and pin up the remainder of the hem to the finished length (at the notch point) and then hand stitch the hem so that the stitching is not visible from the right side); do not topstitch along the centre fronts for this version.

17. Press the top of the pockets to the wrong side by 1 cm (⅜ in.), then press down a second time as far as the notch. Do not press in the curved edges of the pocket bags – instead, keep these edges flat and raw.

Tip: The placement of the pockets is a matter of personal preference, but we find that the chest pocket looks nice with the top edge starting around 23–25 cm (9–10 in.) down from the shoulder. The bottom edges of the hip pockets should start around 5 cm (2 in.) up from the finished hem. Both chest and hip pockets should start 8.5 cm (3½ in.) away from the centre front edges.

18. Hand stitch the turn-downs of the pockets in place, using running stitch and just catching the outer fabric as you go.

19. Sew a ruffle around the side and bottom edges of the pocket, with the centre of the ruffle about 1 cm (⅜ in.) away from the raw edges. Fold under an extra length of ruffle at the start and finish point (the top left and right side of the pocket) to neaten it at the top.

20. Pin the pockets in place and topstitch them to the jacket, sewing through the centre of the ruffle that was attached in step 19.

21. Sew buttons and horizontal buttonholes on the centre fronts. The first buttonhole should be placed about 2.5 cm (1 in.) down from the top, with three more spaced about 15 cm (6 in.) apart below it.

METHOD:

COLLAGE

The collage method encompasses a few different techniques. We love it, as it's extremely versatile and a great way to use up all your random-sized pieces, and even your smaller tiny scraps.

Here we take you through three ways of working with the collage method. The application method varies from project to project, but the thing that ties them all together is the fact that they all need to be placed on a fabric base of some sort. Essentially, this method involves adding textile decoration and texture to another piece of fabric or garment.

Option A: Appliqué Motif is the act of applying a pre-planned design or motif to a garment.

Option B: Appliqué Surface involves applying random-sized fabric offcuts to a base to make an entirely new fabric.

Option C: Terrazzo is similar to option B but uses tiny scraps all blended together to make a new textile surface

RE-MAKE JEANS

PIECE VEST

TERRAZZO CLUTCH

RE-MAKE JUMPER

LOGO TEE

CHOOSING FABRICS

The fabrics you choose for this can vary greatly, and the sizes depend on the design you are applying. For options A and B (appliqué), it's a good idea to use fabrics that are relatively stable (silky, slippery fabrics can be hard to work with). Choose, for example, cottons and linens and any other stable fabrics. The weights can vary, but think about the surface you are applying the appliqué to. For example, if you are applying appliqué decoration to a light-weight cotton jersey you should choose appliqué fabrics that are not too thick. Refer to the individual projects for more detailed info on fabric choices. For option C (terrazzo), you can use any weight of fabric and in particular all those small, bitty pieces that are hard to find a use for anywhere else.

Once you have learnt the basic steps, you can then try them out in the following projects:

- Re-make Jumper, page 156 (skill level 1)
- Re-make Jeans, page 162 (skill level 1)
- Logo Tee, page 168 (skill level 1)
- Piece Vest, page 174 (skill level 3)
- Terrazzo Clutch, page 182 (skill level 2–3)

OPTION A: APPLIQUÉ MOTIF

This option shows you how to apply a pre-planned design to a garment using fabric scraps. You can use this method sparingly, as we have done in the Logo Tee where one design is applied to a T-shirt, or you can cover an entire garment to make an appliqué 'print'. The fabric 'motifs' are placed directly onto the garment you are working with and sewn in place by machine, using either straight stitch or zig-zag.

1. Draw the motifs you want to use on paper templates and cut them out. (In this book we have provided the Cloud motifs for the Re-make Jumper, page 156, and the Planet motif for the Logo Tee, page 168.) Draw around the templates on your chosen fabric and cut out the shapes.

2. Pin the fabric motifs in place on your garment, then attach them using your sewing machine. We are showing two options for this:

   (a) Straight stitch with raw edges: Straight stitch all around about 0.8-1 cm (¼–⅜ in.) away from the raw edges. The edges will fray over time, creating a soft look.

   (b) Zig-zag: Sew around all edges using zig-zag stitch. Make sure that the zig-zag is wide enough to cover the raw edges and secure all the threads so that the pieces do not fray.

Tips:

Make sure your designs are not too thin and tiny, as they will be difficult to sew.

If you are using a couple of different shapes and fabrics, try to overlap the pieces slightly where they meet (this can be seen in the way the Planet motif is applied).

If you are using a light-weight fabric with a bit of stretch in it, it is very helpful (but not always essential) to secure the motif and a small piece of backing fabric in an embroidery hoop before machining it in place on the garment.

If your appliqué pieces are moving around a lot, tack them to the garment before machining them in place.

OPTION B: APPLIQUÉ SURFACE

This option is a way of building up a new fabric on a base using random-sized offcuts and is a beautiful way to use up odd-shaped scraps. When using similar-coloured fabrics, it creates a garment that is textured yet very wearable. However, this method is also super fun and playful when you combine pop colours to make the collage surface. The fabric scraps can be sewn by hand or by machine.

1. Choose the fabric scraps you want to use and plan out your appliqué surface on a fabric base. Here we are using a base that consists of a cotton lining and a layer of wadding, and we are building up the appliqué pieces on top of the wadding. This layer will be the outer (right) side of the garment when finished.

2. Make sure that all the pieces you want to use are overlapped by at least 2.5 cm (1 in.). This ensures that once you sew on the scraps there will not be any gaps exposing the base fabric underneath.

3. Pin your scraps in place through all layers.

4. Baste the scraps in place by working long running stitches around the shapes, sewing through all layers about 5 mm (¼ in.) away from the raw edges.

5. Finally, stitch the scraps down through all layers, using hand running stitch or machine zig-zag stitch. On the right, you can see an example of a hand-stitched version, where the entire piece of fabric has been covered in stitches, creating stability but also a beautiful texture throughout. The second example in navy shows the pieces attached with machine zig-zag stitch around all edges.

1.

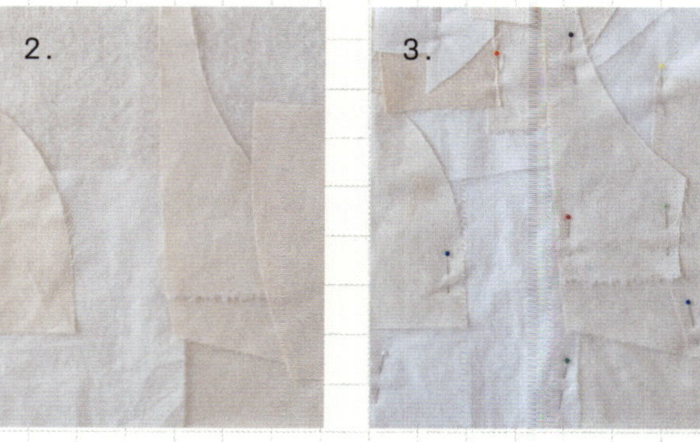
2. 3.

4.

5.

OPTION C: TERRAZZO

This method is a way of using all the tiny little leftover fabric scraps that are always so hard to find a use for. The modern method of tiled terrazzo dates back to the 1500s, when Venetian mosaic workers created it as a way of using up all the little crushed-up bits of waste. We therefore thought the name Terrazzo Textiles was apt.

1. Make a card template to use as an aid when sewing on the scraps. Make sure the card is not too thick – something like an old cereal box is perfect. Cut a strip about 5 x 45 cm (2 x 18 in.).

2. Prepare the fabric base you would like to use. Here, because our example is the Terrazzo Clutch (page 182), we have used a layer of lining fabric with a cotton wadding on top, which will add structure and stability to the piece. Once you have cut your base fabrics to size, tack them together in a few spots just to hold them in place.

3. Plan in which direction you want to stitch down your fabric scraps. Here we are going to stitch the pieces down in diagonal lines. We also marked out guidelines about 10 cm (4 in.) apart for the stitching lines.

4. Now you can begin to place some of the scrappy offcuts on the wadding side, starting in one corner. Place the scraps in a fairly messy way, but still pay attention to the order of colours and textures. Make sure the wadding is not visible under the area you have covered with scraps. Pin the scraps in place in a few spots so that they don't move around too much.

5. Start sewing on the section of scraps using the strip of card you cut in step 1. Place the card under the outer edge of the machine foot on the left as you sew (do not actually sew through it!). This helps to keep the scraps to the left in place as you slowly add lines of stitches. Sew diagonal lines parallel to the lines you marked out in step 2, approximately 1–2 cm (½–¾ in.) apart. The stitching should go through all layers.

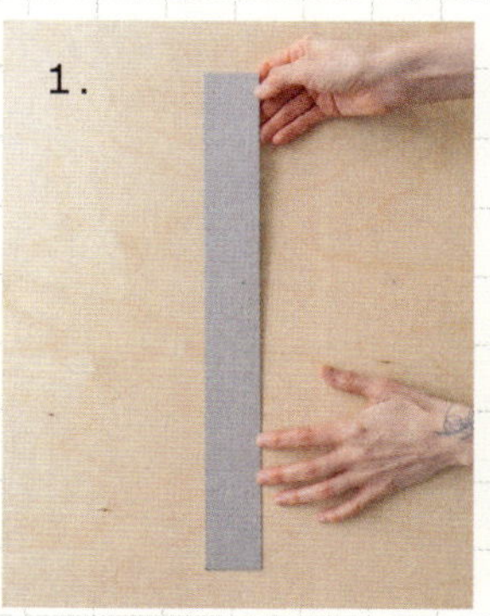

1.

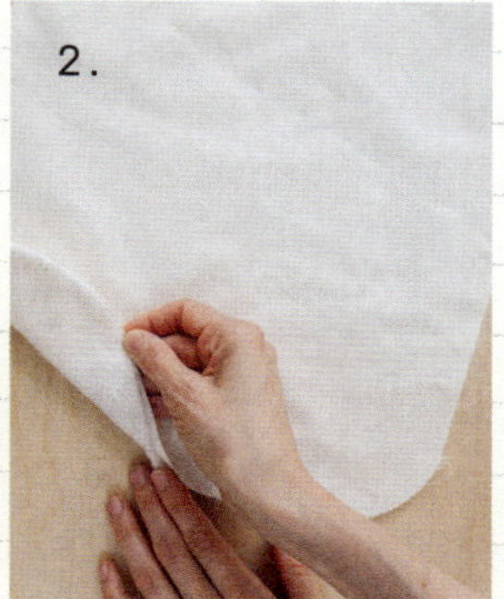

2.

3.

4.

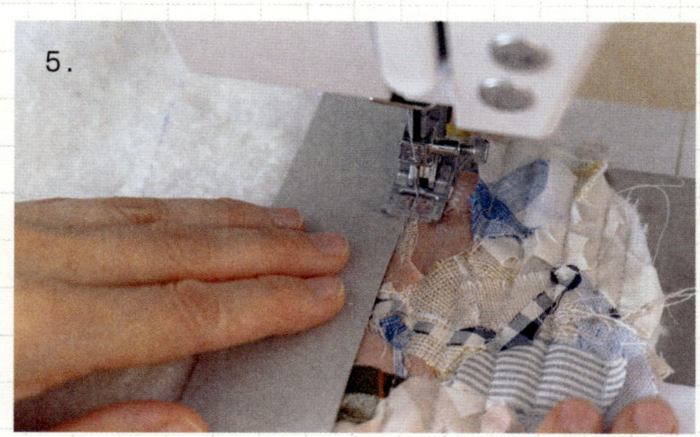

5.

Tip: If you need some extra area to support the fabric you are working with, you can use a table attachment for your sewing machine (this depends on the capabilities of the sewing machine you have), or place something like a pile of books to the left of your machine, as we have done here, to get it to the height you need. This will help to keep your fabric in place while you are sewing.

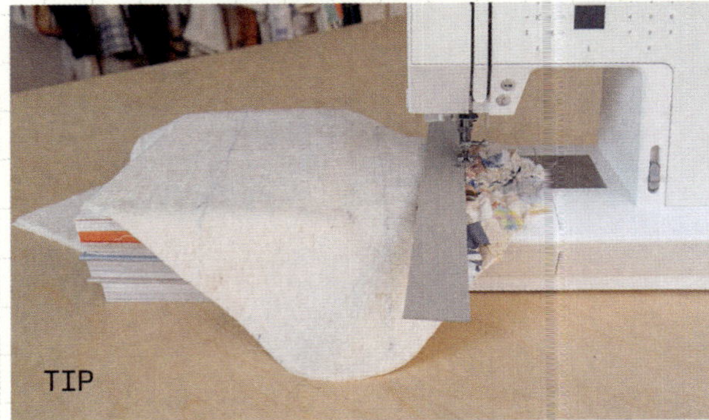
TIP

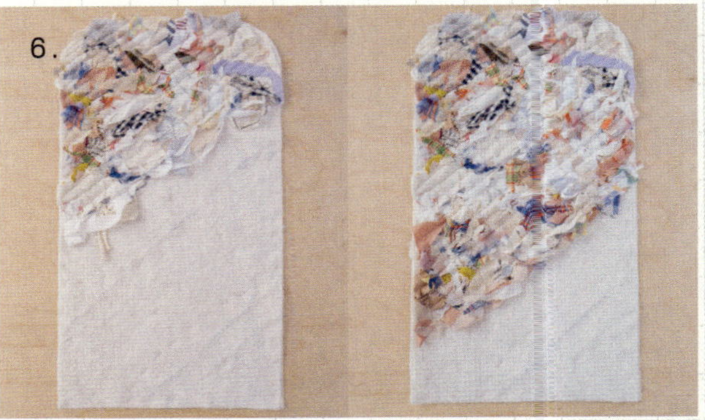
6.

6. Once you have secured the first section in place, you can place more scraps on the wadding, working with a small section at a time, taking it to the machine, sewing the diagonal lines, and repeating until the entire piece is covered.

7. Once the whole piece is covered, go over it with diagonal stitch lines in the other direction, to really hold the scraps neatly in place. You shouldn't need to use your card strip in this final step.

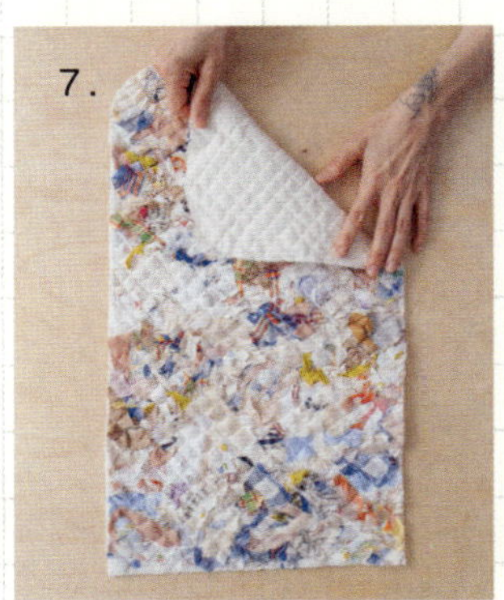
7.

VARIATIONS

Here are a selection of ideas using the collage method, showing different patterns and colours, to help inspire your projects.

OPTION 1:

Zig-zagged appliqué

OPTION 2:

Zig-zagged appliqué with quilting

OPTION 3:

Raw-edge appliqué (coloured motifs)

OPTION 4:

Raw-edge appliqué (tone on tone)

OPTION 5:

Hand-stitched patches (denim mend)

OPTION 6:

Hand-stitched patches (tone on tone)

OPTION 7:

Terrazzo (colour)

OPTION 8:

Terrazzo (dark neutrals)

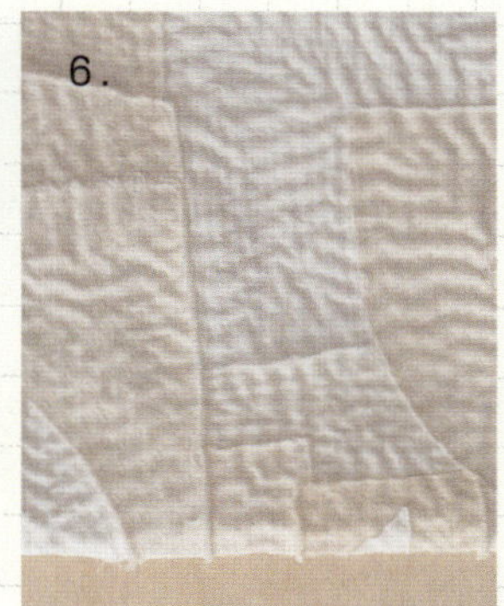

RE-MAKE JUMPER

Skånsk
Larmtjänst
JARI

We began playing around with the idea of patching over stains and holes right back when we first started Helgrose, with a series of re-make white T-shirts, covering old branding and blemishes with black contrast patches. Since then we have explored many different ways of working with this method. We particularly enjoy the concept of making an all-over 'print' with appliqué motifs, which is how we see this application.

You can do a high-contrast appliqué for that 'pop' effect or, if you'd like a more subtle look, try tone on tone, which will add a beautiful all-over texture to the garment. For this project we stitched on all the motifs with straight stitch, leaving raw edges to fray with wash and wear. If you prefer to not have frayed edges, you can attach the appliqué motifs with a zig-zag stitch instead. This is a pretty simple project in which you should really be able to let your creativity go wild. Have fun!

SKILL LEVEL 

TECHNIQUE

Appliqué motif

RE-MAKE GARMENT USED

Second-hand jumper with a few stains scattered across the front and back body. Jumper labelled as S/M, worn by Sarah.

FABRIC

For your re-make garment, we recommend you choose something in a fabric that is relatively stable and not too thin and stretchy – a medium- to heavy-weight jumper fabric works really well. For the appliqué, choose light- to medium-weight scraps that are big enough to cut your motifs from, ideally cotton and linen.

TEMPLATES

We have provided the cloud templates we used for this project in three sizes. If you want to make your own motifs, use simple shapes that aren't too hard to sew, such as the tiles example in option 4 on page 155, which are simple rectangles cut all the same size.

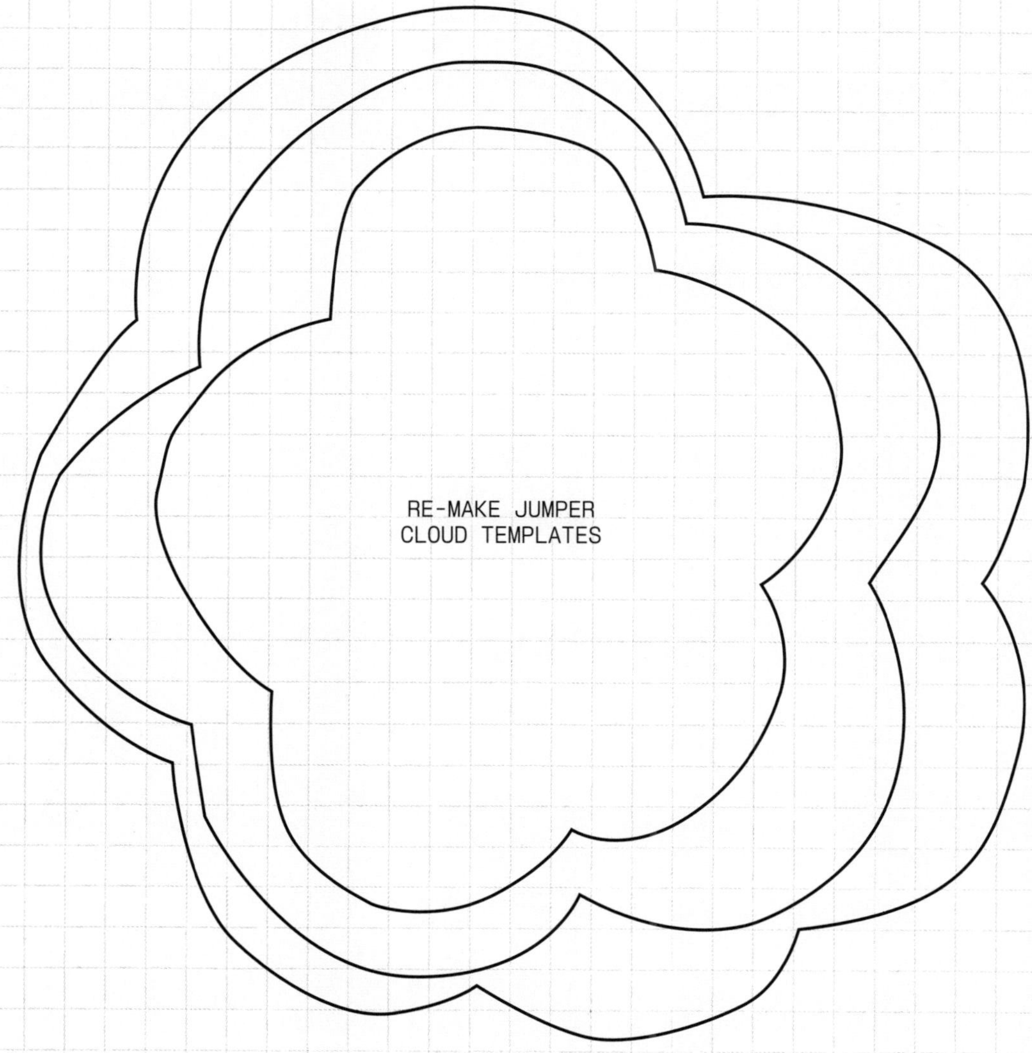

METHOD

PREPARING THE APPLIQUÉ MOTIFS

Decide which fabrics you want to use and choose offcuts that will be big enough for one of the three shapes. For this project, we used four different fabrics and cut the same number of each template size and fabric type (the total amount of cut shapes will depend on how big your garment is).

PREPARING THE JUMPER

1. Turn the jumper inside out and cut off the underarm (photo 1a) and side seams, so that you can open out your garment and lay it flat (photo 1b). Try to remove as little fabric as possible from each seam.

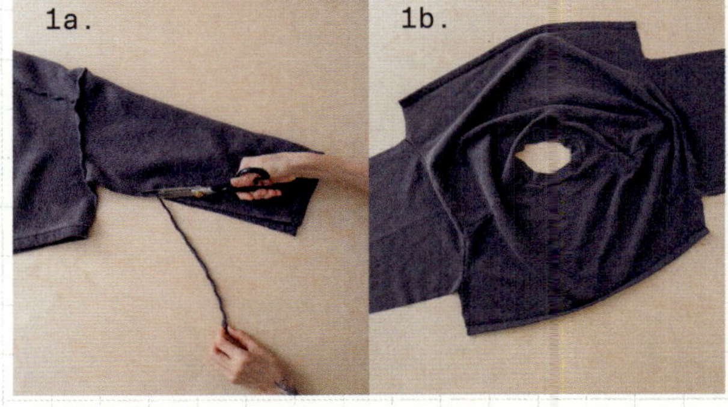

<u>Tip:</u> If you don't want to reduce the size of the garment too much, you can unpick the seams instead.

2. Place your appliqué motifs on top of the jumper, spreading them out evenly, with alternating fabric types. It should look a bit like an all-over print.

3. Sew on the motifs, stitching about 0.8–1 cm (¼–⅜ in.) away from the raw edges (see page 151).

4. Once all of your motifs have been sewn on, place the front and back body pieces right sides together and pin the body and underarm seams, matching the underarm points and the finished edges on the sleeve and body hems. Sew together with a 4-thread overlocker, leaving an extra 3-cm (1¼-in.) length of overlocking on each end. (Alternatively, use straight stitch and overlock the seam allowances together.) Press the seams towards the back, then turn your overlocking tail inside the seam and topstitch it down to finish the sleeve and body hems neatly.

RE-MAKE JEANS

These are a favourite pair of old vintage Levi jeans that Birgitta has had for over 10 years. They were even styled with some pieces in her last book, *Zero Waste Patterns*! Two years on, they have gotten quite worn and thin in areas and she wanted to find a way to get more life out of them. This method is inspired by vintage Japanese mending and the patches we used were taken from various places, including denim from the sleeves cut off from the Re-make Jacket project on page 76, as well as offcuts from our daughter's jeans (she made a cute pair of shorts when her favourite jeans got too worn out!).

This project is great for beginners although it does involve a bit of hand stitching, so be patient – the results are well worth it! We hope you can use it as inspiration to see what sort of textures you can create while extending the life of some of your most-loved clothes.

SKILL LEVEL ●○○○○

TECHNIQUE

Appliqué surface

RE-MAKE GARMENT USED

Vintage Levi jeans with holes and large areas of thinning fabric across the front thighs and knees. Worn by Anti.

FABRIC

Assorted cotton scraps for patches in medium- to heavy-weight cotton.

NOTIONS

Hand sewing needle and thread (ideally 100% cotton thread, as you are covering much of the fabric and this will be the softest and match the existing fabric content).

METHOD

PREPARING THE JEANS

Prepare your jeans by unpicking the side seams on both sides, as far up as the damaged areas go, making sure you stop unpicking at least 5 cm (2 in.) before you get to a potential metal stud (often found in the pockets of jeans and other areas). You will also need to unpick about 5 cm (2 in.) of the hems near the side seam on each side of the jeans.

PREPARING THE JEANS

PLANNING YOUR PATCHES

1. Choose a few different fabrics that look nice on the re-make garment you are working with. Here we chose fabrics that blend in quite tonally with the main fabric of the jeans, so that the mending is a little more subtle. We used denim offcuts as well as some medium-weight cotton twill.

2. Place the patchwork pieces across the areas you wish to mend, making sure you allow for extra around areas where the fabric is getting quite thin, as this will ensure that the mending job is strong and will last a lot longer with wash and wear. Cut all the patches to size, making sure you cut along the straight grain or weft so that you have nice straight square or rectangular pieces. You can even overlap some pieces here and there, as long as the fabrics aren't too thick.

3. Once you have planned out the patches and pinned them in place, baste each one onto the jeans, sewing around each patch about 1 cm (⅜ in.) away from the raw edges.

2.

4. Now cover all your patches with running hand stitch (see page 152); the stitches should be no more than about 5–8 mm (¼–⅜ in.) long so that the threads don't get too loopy (photo 4a). The stitches should run vertically down the garment (along the grainline) and the rows should be around 5-8 mm (¼–⅜ in.) apart (photo 4b, showing the inside of the garment). If you want to keep your lines as straight as possible, you can draw a few vertical guidelines to help you keep on track, using chalk or a dissolvable fabric marker pen.

5. Once all the patches have been covered with stitching, pull out all the tacking stitches, and then sew the side seams of the jeans back together, using the same seam allowance as on the original garment. Overlock (or zig-zag) the seams together to stop the raw edges from fraying. Finally, stitch up the hem where required. If you can match the original thread, go for it – otherwise use a natural-looking thread, as we have done here.

LOGO TEE

A while back we started branding our tees and jumpers with appliqué motifs and Helgrose logos using leftover scraps, each one a little different from the next. It's a great way to personalize and give character to an otherwise plain garment. This project can be made as a new tee that you add appliqué to. Alternatively, you could start at step 9 and give new life to an old tee by simply adding appliqué to cover worn-out logos or stains. We have provided our planet motif for you to use, but hope you get creative and design your own motifs too. The world is your oyster with this one – just remember to use shapes that aren't too complicated or small, so that the motifs are not too difficult to sew on.

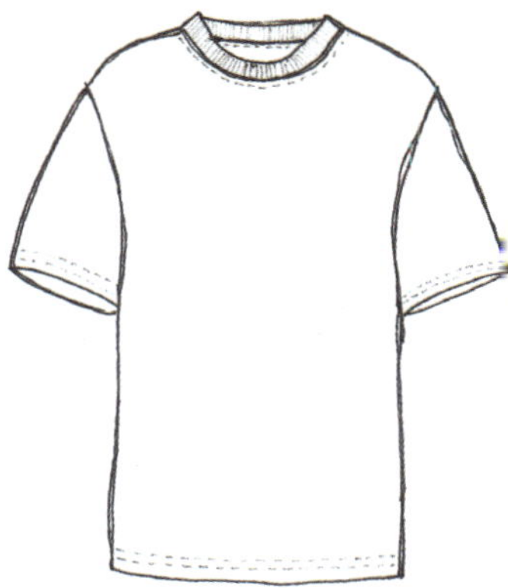

SKILL LEVEL ●○○○○

TECHNIQUE

Appliqué motif

SIZE MADE

Size S/M worn by Anti

FABRIC

For this project we have used a colour-grown* organic cotton jersey to make the tee and an organic cotton ribbing for the neck. For the appliqué motifs, we used light-weight cotton scraps.

*Colour-grown cotton means that the yarn has not been dyed. It is, in fact, the actual colour of the cotton grown.

NOTIONS

2 x 1 organic cotton ribbing – refer to neckband pattern piece D for cut size.

Tip: Sew the tee using a 4-thread overlocker. Alternatively, use stretch stitch and a ballpoint needle with a 7–8-mm (a generous ¼-in.) seam allowance and then overlock or zig-zag the seam allowances together.

ADDITIONAL TOOLS

An embroidery hoop may be useful for certain fabrics – for example, stretch – as this will keep the fabric stable as you sew on the appliqué. When using a hoop, check the diameter size will fit in your sewing machine.

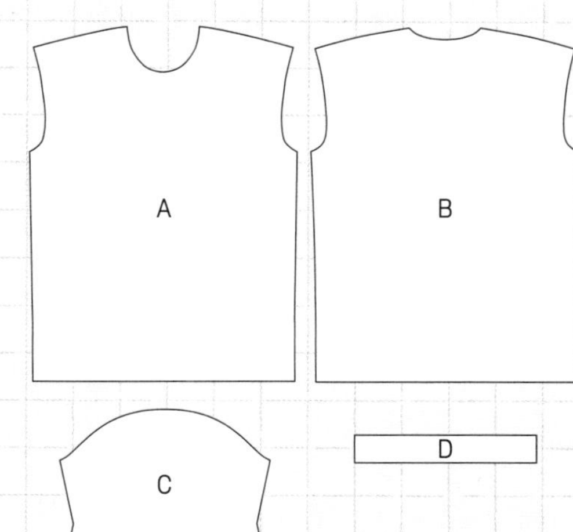

PATTERN

You will need the following pattern pieces from the Tee pattern. Refer to the layout plans in How to use this book, page 17, for the best layout plan on your fabric based on your chosen size.

- A: Front – cut 1 in jersey
- B: Back – cut 1 in jersey
- C: Sleeve – cut 1 pair in jersey
- D: Neckband – cut 1 in ribbing

TEMPLATES

We have provided the planet templates that we used for this project, but if you want to make your own motifs, use simple shapes that aren't too hard to sew. Trace the round planet (1) and the ring (2) as separate templates, and cut them from different fabrics. The shaded areas indicate how the outer edges of the ring (2) should slot underneath the planet (1) when sewn onto the Tee.

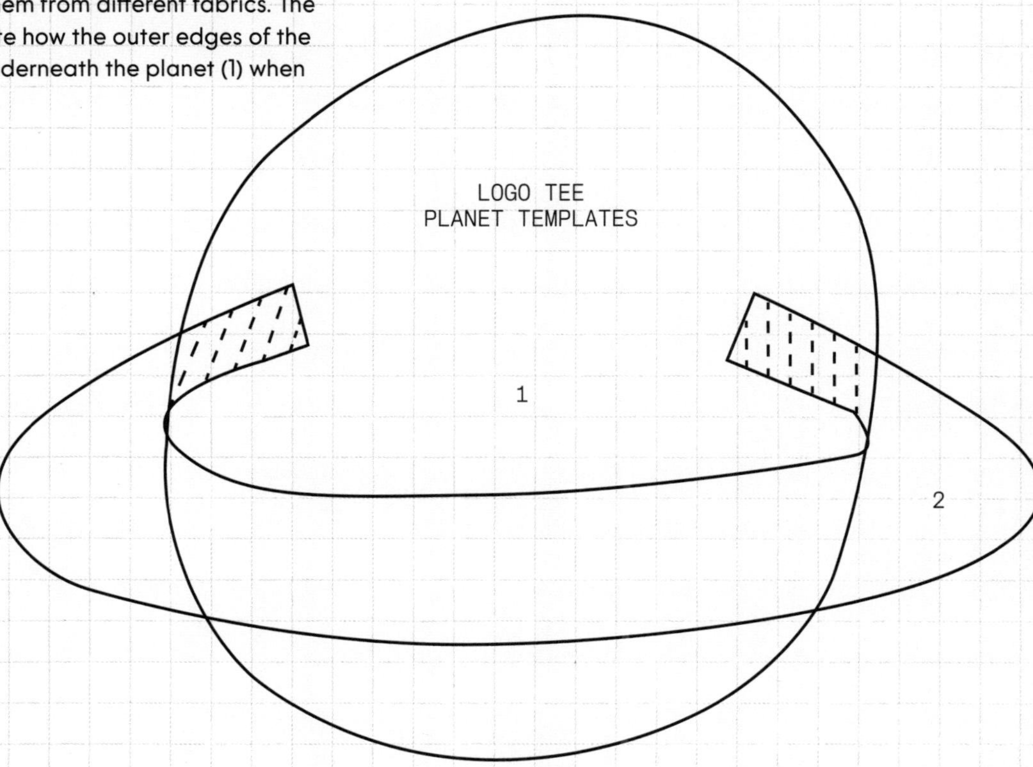

METHOD

PREPARING THE APPLIQUÉ MOTIFS

1. Trace the templates for the planet and its ring onto paper and cut them out.

2. Use the paper templates to cut one planet and its ring from your chosen fabric scraps.

SEWING

1. Place the front and back body pieces right sides together and sew the shoulder seams. Press the seams towards the back.

2. With right sides together, matching the shoulder notch on the sleeves to the shoulder seams on the body, sew the sleeve heads into the armholes. Press the seams down into the sleeve.

3. With right sides together, sew the underarm and side seams in one continuous line of stitching on each side from the sleeve hem to the body hem. Press the seams towards the back.

4. Fold the neck ribbing in half, right sides together, matching the short ends. Sew the centre back seam and press the seam open.

5. Press the neckband in half as shown, wrong sides together, then machine baste the long raw edges together, keeping your stitches within the seam allowance.

6. Matching the centre back seam of the neckband to the centre back neck notch, and matching the centre front notches together, pin the raw edges of the neckband to the neckline, stretching the band out evenly around the neck. Starting at one of the shoulders, sew the band all the way around with a 4-thread overlocker (or use straight stitch and overlock the seams together). Press the seams into the body.

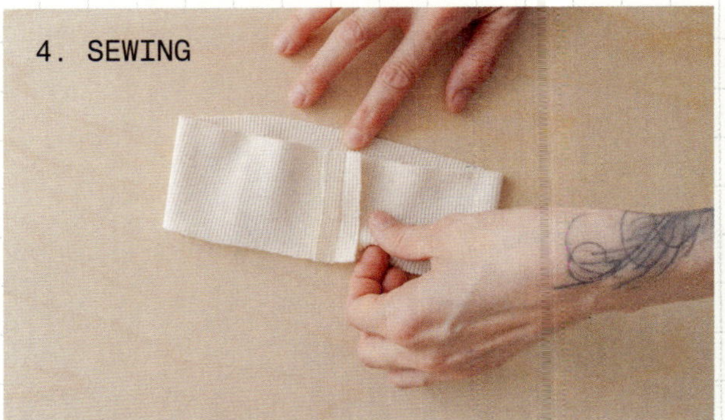

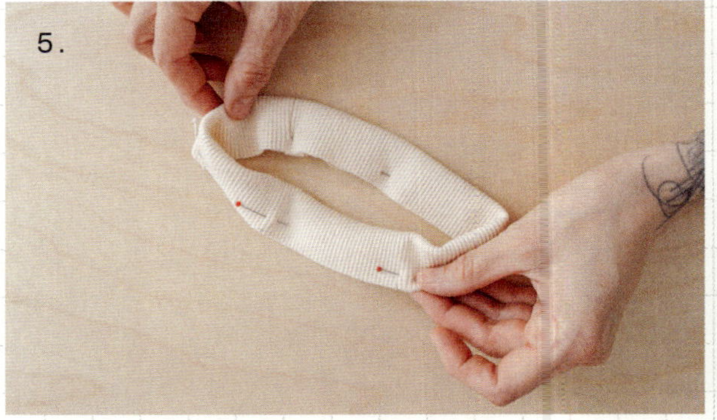

7. We also added topstitching (optional) in a contrast thread around the neck as a detail, sewn close the edge of the seam around the body section (not on the ribbed band).

8. Overlock the raw edges of the sleeve and body hems. Press the hems to the wrong side by 3 cm (1¼ in.). Sew the hems down with two rows of straight stitching, using a twin needle if you have one.

9. Try on the garment and decide roughly where you want the appliqué to sit. A good position is usually around chest height, halfway between the centre front and the side seam of the garment. Mark the position with tailor's chalk or a dissolvable fabric marker pen. Place the appliqué over this mark and pin in place, in the order that the different appliqué elements need to go – see Tip, right. If you wish, you can tack the appliqué pieces to hold them securely in place before machine stitching.

10. Now put the embroidery hoop around the area for appliqué, if you are using a fabric that requires this (photo 10a). As we used a fairly light-weight jersey for the tee, we also added an extra layer of scrap jersey fabric on the wrong side for extra strength, securing it neatly with the embroidery hoop (photo 10b). Sew the appliqué down by zig-zag stitching around all raw edges (see page 151).

11. If you used a backing fabric for support, you can now neatly cut away any excess on the back, leaving around 8 mm (¼ in.) extra fabric around all edges (photo 11a). Now give the appliqué motif a good steam with your iron, and you are done (photo 11b)!

7.

8.

Tip: Note that the outer edges of piece 2 should be placed under piece 1 for a neat finish. These areas are shaded on template 2.

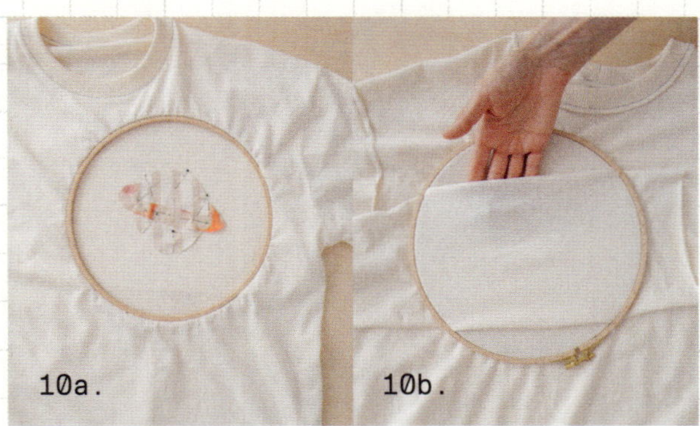
10a. 10b.

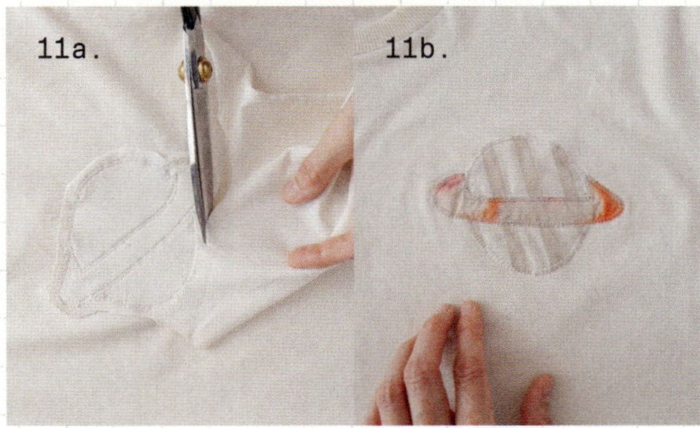
11a. 11b.

PIECE VEST

This quilted vest is pieced together using odd-shaped fabric offcuts from the production of other garments – hence the name Piece Vest! Sam kept it for himself and has literally not taken it off – that's how we know it's a winner. The wadding adds an extra level of warmth, making it a great layer for winter or a perfect outer garment for summer evenings.

As this vest is made in similar tones, it is really wearable and relatively understated – but we can't wait to see some being made in loud, lairy, pop colours. It uses the Tee pattern as a base (no sleeves) and has a relaxed fit and slightly dropped shoulder. We used a rouleau tie as a closure, but it would look just as great with a button closure. However you choose to make it, you will certainly end up with a personalized piece that'll be a great addition to your summer/winter wardrobe. Dive in!

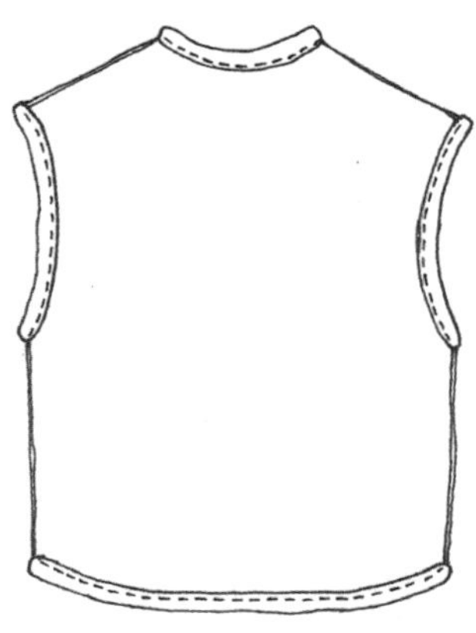

SKILL LEVEL ●●●○○

TECHNIQUE

Appliqué surface

SIZE MADE

L/XL worn by Ludjero

FABRIC

For this project we used a light-weight navy linen for the lining (we patchworked our lining together using various-sized offcuts). The wadding is an organic cotton/recycled poly, and the outer is pieced from cotton corduroy and linen offcuts in random shapes.

NOTIONS

- Bias binding, 2.5cm (1 in.) wide x 60 cm (24 in.) long, in a light-weight cotton or linen, for the rouleau ties.
- Bias binding, 4 cm (1½ in.) wide x 420 cm (165 in.) long, to bind the neck, hems and armholes; the length may vary slightly depending on what size you're making.

PATTERN

The Piece Vest is made using the Tee pattern as a base. You will need the following pattern pieces:

- A: Front
- B: Back

You will also need the Workwear Jacket chest pocket pattern (I).

<u>Pattern adjustments</u>

1. Follow the shoulder, centre front, hem and armhole line for the Vest on the front Tee pattern piece (A).
2. Follow the shoulder, hem and armhole line for the Vest on the back Tee pattern piece (B).

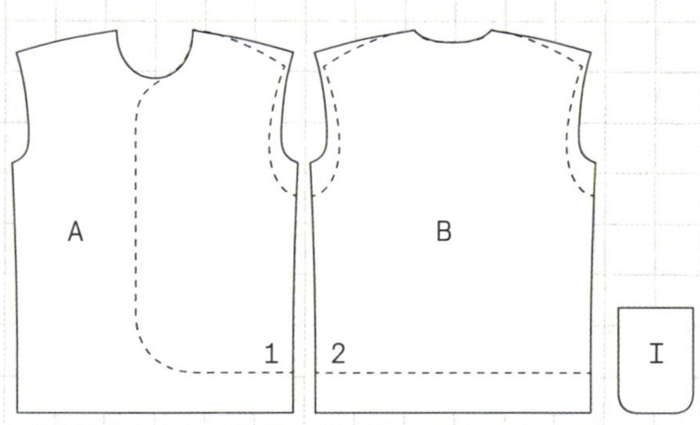

LAYOUT PLANS

Start by cutting a set of wadding pieces and a set of lining pieces using the same pattern pieces. All the required pattern pieces have been arranged in layouts showing how to determine the amount of fabric you need and the most efficient way to cut the pattern pieces.

To determine the finished fabric sizes you need for the wadding and lining, lay your paper pattern pieces out as shown here. Measure the width and length for the total amount of fabric you need for each layout. Cut the required pieces from the wadding and lining fabric.

Wadding layout plan

- A: Front – cut 1 pair
- B: Back – cut 1

Lining fabric layout plan

Use either fabric off the roll or patchwork together your lining to the required size using light-weight pieces of fabric.

- A: Front – cut 1 pair
- B: Back – cut 1

Outer fabric

- I: Chest pocket* – cut 1

*This should be cut from a piece of fabric used for the outer 'collage' part of your vest. You can either cut it from one whole piece of fabric or patchwork together several small pieces to reach the desired size.

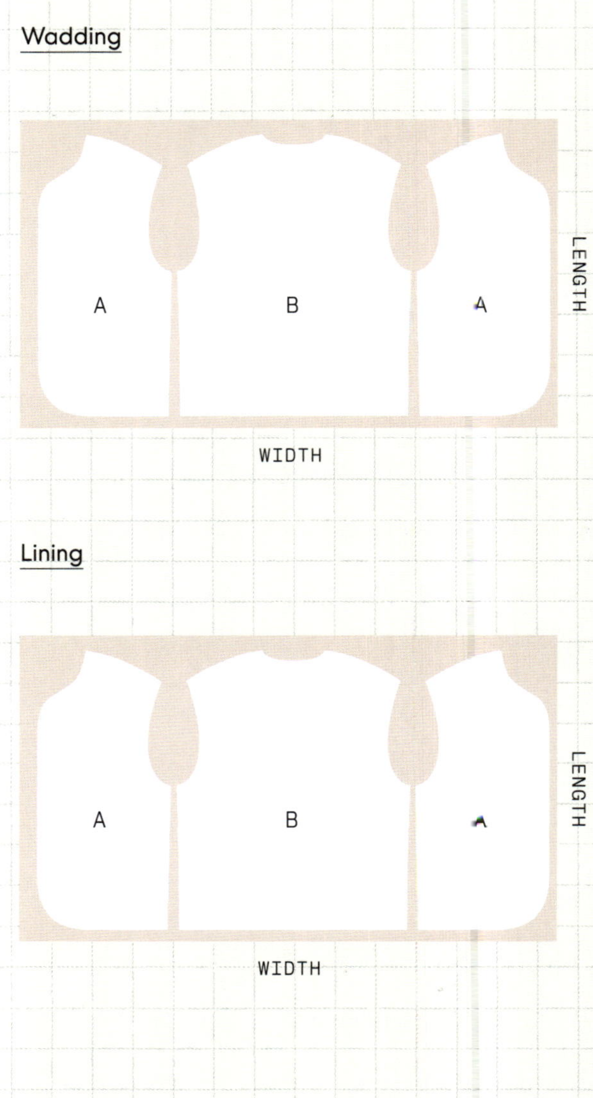

METHOD

PREPARING THE OUTER FABRIC

Collect a heap of scraps you would like to use for your outer fabric; they shouldn't be too small, as you will be stitching all the pieces on by zig-zagging around the raw edges. We put together fabrics that are similar colours, but if you are mixing different colours try to avoid combining both dark and light in case the colours bleed.

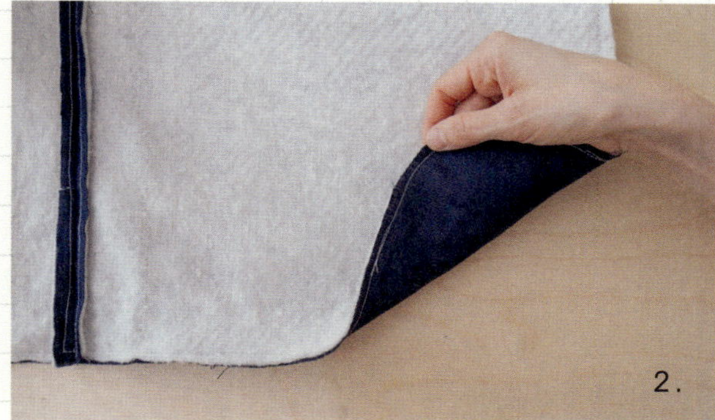
2.

> <u>Note:</u> All seam allowances are 1 cm (⅜ in.) unless otherwise stated.

3.

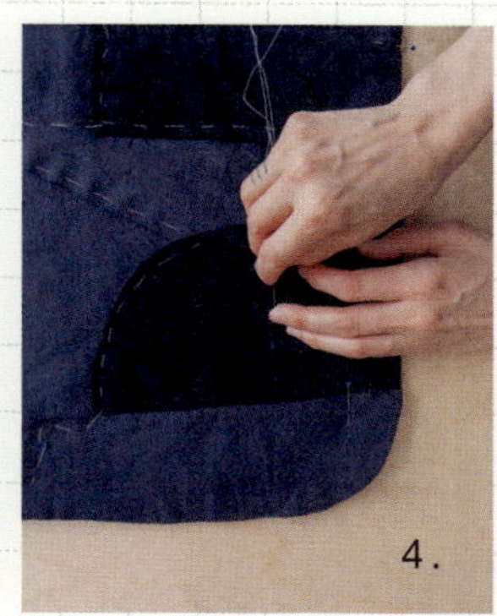
4.

SEWING

1. Sew the lining pieces to the wadding, with the wrong side of the lining against the wadding, stitching all around about 8 mm (¼ in.) away from the raw edges. Make sure the fabric and wadding are nice and flat when sewn.

2. Place the lining sides of the front and back together. Sew the side seams, then press the seams open.

3. Place the random-sized offcuts on the wadding side to build up your outer fabric, overlapping all pieces by at least 2.5 cm (1 in.) to ensure that no wadding will peek through later, until the vest is completely covered, continuing the patchwork over the side seams; you can use both small and large pieces to do this and cut to the required size where needed.

4. Pin the offcuts in place and tack around all the raw edges, stitching through all layers, to hold the pieces in place. Trim off any excess at the armholes, neck and hem so that the outer layer is level with the wadding/lining.

5. Zig-zag stitch around all the raw edges, through all layers (see page 151).

6. Using a sharp piece of tailor's chalk or a dissolvable fabric marker pen, draw diagonal quilting lines across the vest in both directions, spacing them 8 cm (about 3 in.) apart. Roll up the fabric diagonally from one corner and sew the quilting lines in one direction through all layers (see page 31). Repeat with the diagonal lines going in the other direction.

7. Bind the front and back shoulders (see page 37), pinning and stitching the binding to the wrong (lining) side of the vest first.

8. With right sides together, sew the front and back shoulders together. Press the seams open.

9. Bind the armholes. Start at the back near the side seam and fold in the end of the binding by about 1 cm (⅜ in.), to the binding side. Pin the binding to the wrong (lining) side of the vest first (photo 9a) and sew all the way around, overlapping the ends by about 1.5 cm/⅝ in. (photo 9b). Turn the binding to the front by folding it over twice by about 1 cm (⅜ in.) each time. Pin it in place and topstitch to finish (photo 9c, opposite, top).

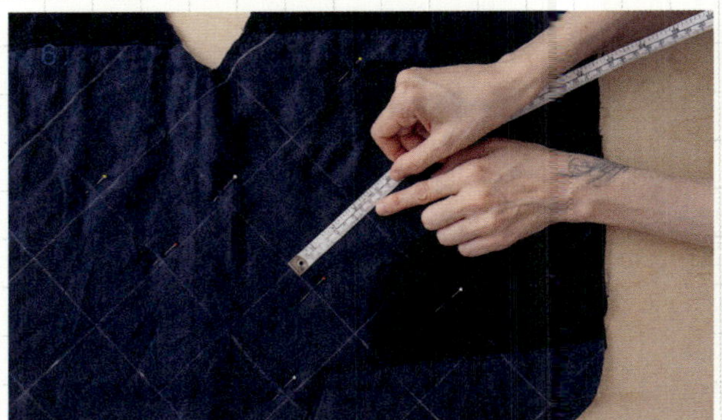

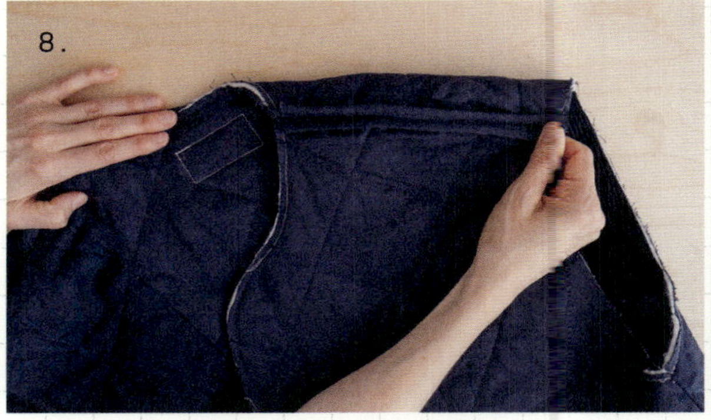

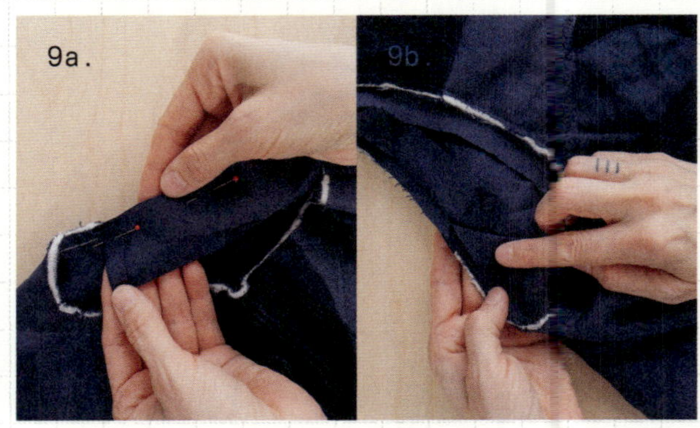

10. Cut the 2.5-cm (1-in.) binding in half, so that you have two 30-cm (12-in.) lengths. Sew the rouleau ties (see page 30). Pin one end of one tie to the lining side of the right centre front edge approximately 37 cm (14½ in.) down from the shoulder, or to your preference. The tie should be pointing towards the side seam. Stitch the tie in place. Tie a knot on the raw end of the tie and trim off the excess.

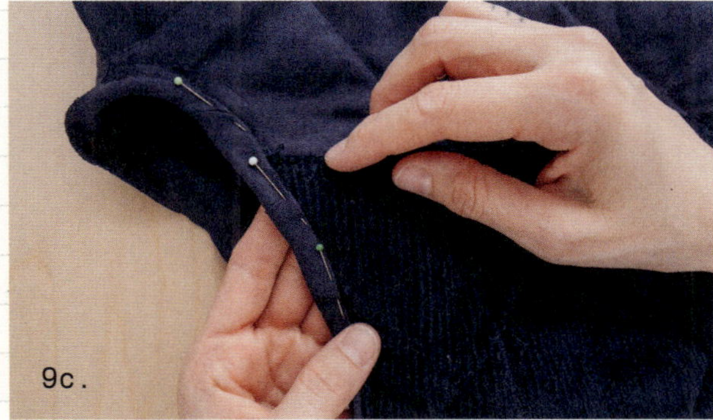
9c.

11. Bind the neck and hems, all in one go. Start at the back hem, close to one side seam, and fold in the end of the binding, as in step 9. Once the binding is fully attached all the way around, pull the tie out to the centre front, so that it's now facing away from the vest, and topstitch to secure it to the outer edge of the binding.

12.

12. Prepare the patch pocket, pin it in place on the right-hand side of the vest, and topstitch it down (see page 37). For size L/XL, the pocket looked nice placed about 25 cm (10 in.) down from the shoulder seam and 7 cm (2¾ in.) in from the centre front edge.

13. Cut a 4 x 6-cm (1½ –2½-in.) piece of leftover binding and press all four edges to the wrong side by about 8 mm (¼ in.), to make a little rectangle. Place the remaining rouleau tie on the left front, lining it up with the tie on the right front. The start of the tie should be attached about 10 cm (4 in.) away from the centre front edge, on the outside of the vest. Secure the tie in place with a few stitches, then place the little rectangle on top to neatly cover the raw end of the tie and topstitch the rectangle down, close to the fold lines, around all edges and through all layers.

TERRAZZO CLUTCH

This is one of our favourite pieces in the book because it is made using all the tiny little leftover scraps from the other projects. We were first inspired to try this technique after seeing a similar method done by Cassandra Belanger of The Stitchery Studio and Lydia Morrow of What Lydia Made, who came up with this wonderful way of using small leftover scraps to make new fabric. At first glance it is the mass of colours that grabs your attention, but the real hero element of this piece is the weighty structure and texture created by the combination of lining, wadding and the terrazzo scrap outer layer. It's really something special.

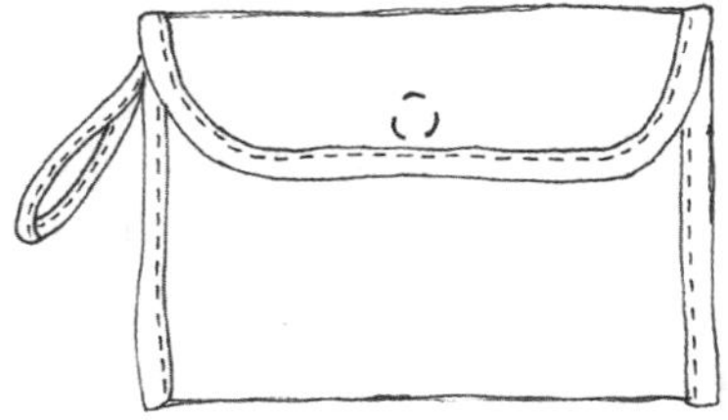

This method shines as a clutch to hold all your daily essentials, but you could adjust the size and use it to store a tablet or laptop as the structure of the finished fabric is very protective and strong. The method would also work beautifully in certain outerwear garments such as a waistcoat/vest (which is what we will be trying next!) or even in some upholstery applications. Really, the limit is simply how far your imagination will take you.

SKILL LEVEL ●●○○○ – ●●●○○

The construction is quite simple, but the terrazzo surface can be a little fiddly to put together.

TECHNIQUE

Terrazzo

SIZE MADE

The finished clutch is 32 cm (12½ in.) wide by 23 cm (9 in.) long.

FABRIC

Assorted small cotton scraps saved from other projects for the terrazzo; any weights will work. Light- to medium-weight cotton for the lining. Cotton wadding for the middle layer.

NOTIONS

- Bias binding, 7.5 cm (3 in.) wide by 130 cm (50 in.), to finish the outer edges. This can be cut from a leftover piece of fabric and sewn together to make the length required.
- 1 sew-on press stud, 25–30 mm (1–1¼ in.) in diameter.
- 5 x 45 cm (2 x 18 in.) light- to medium-weight card (ideally something like a cereal box) to use as an aid for sewing the scraps to the base.

PATTERN

There's no pattern – just cut the pieces following the instructions. The template for the curved end of the clutch is shown below.

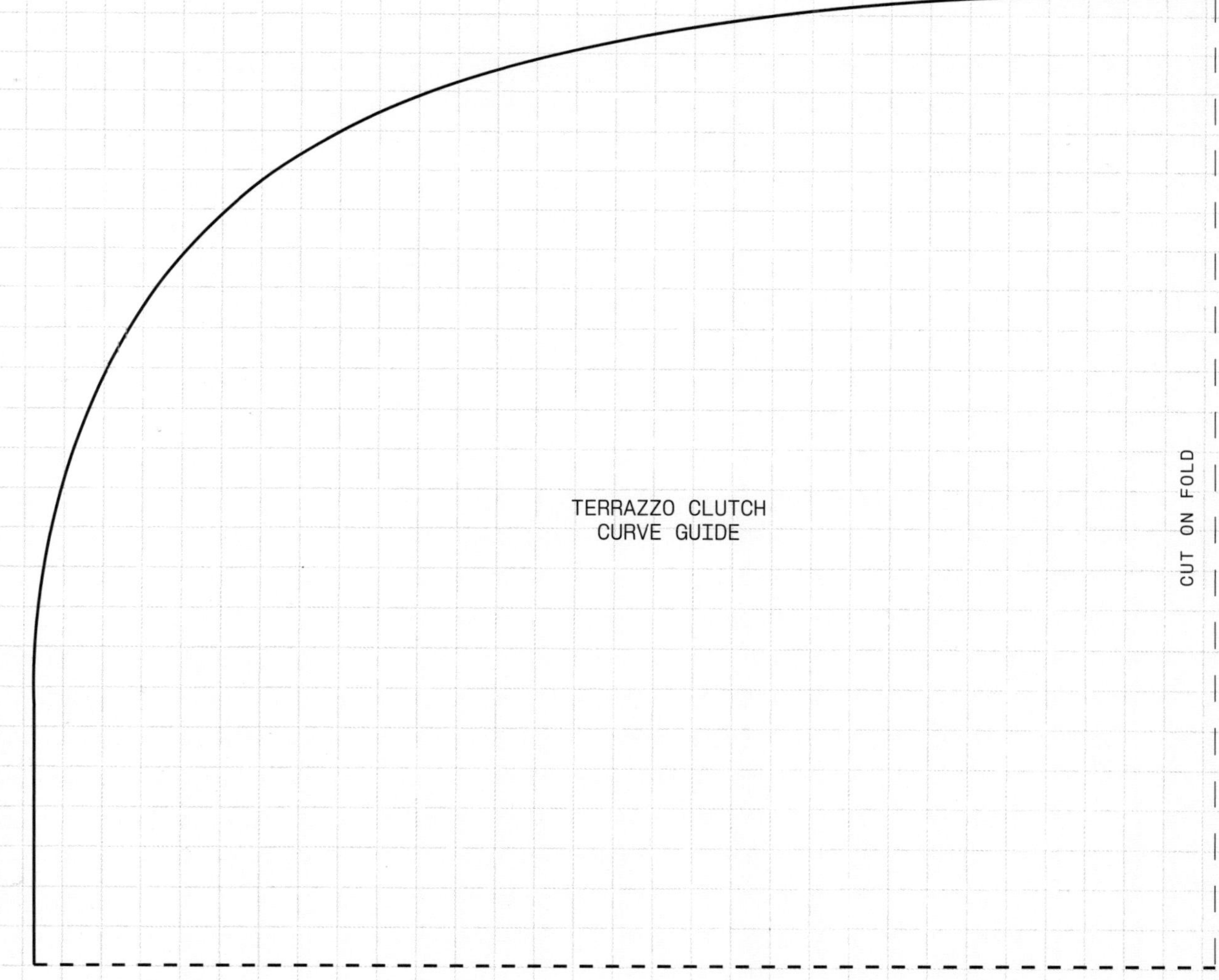

METHOD

CUTTING THE LINING AND WADDING

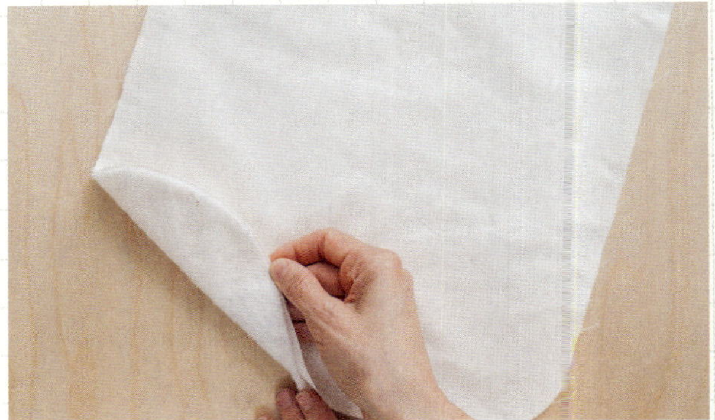

Cut a piece of lining fabric and a piece of wadding measuring 32 x 55 cm (12½ x 21½ in.). Cut a curve on one short end of both pieces, using the template on page 185. Baste the two pieces together.

PREPARING THE OUTER FABRIC

Sort your offcuts into piles of colours and textures that you think look good together. If you have a few bigger scraps, cut them up to match the overall look.

Note: All seam allowances are 1.5 cm (⅝ in.) unless otherwise stated.

SEWING

1.

2a. 2b.

1. Attach the small scraps to the wadding side of your base fabric, following the instructions on pages 153–154.

2. Attach a length of binding to the short straight edge. Pin and sew it from the wrong side first, with a 1.5-cm (⅝-in.) seam allowance (photo 2a), then fold the binding to the right side twice, pin it securely and topstitch it neatly in place along the folded edge (photo 2b).

3. This step is optional, but it's nice to add a little wrist loop, making it easier to carry the clutch when you are out. Cut a straight piece of fabric measuring 4 x 40 cm (1½ x 16 in.) from a scrap you have lying around (we used a medium-weight cotton twill). Press both long edges to the wrong side by about 1 cm (⅜ in.), then press the strip in half and topstitch along each long edge to close and hold in place. Fold the finished strip in half, matching the ends together for make a loop.

4. Pin the loop to the wrong side of one long side, about 40 cm (16 in.) up from the bottom straight edge or just underneath where the flap will be. The loop should face into the clutch. Fold the straight edge of the cluch up by about 20 cm (8 in.), wrong sides together, making sure the wrist loop is sandwiched between the layers. Sew the side seams. (The wrist loop will be stored neatly inside the clutch, but you can slip it out of the top of the clutch when you wish to use it.)

5. Leaving 2 cm (⅜ in.) extra at the start and finish, starting at the bottom folded edge, pin binding around the sides and curved end, as shown. Sew in place with a 1.5-cm (⅝-in.) seam allowance.

6. Fold the excess binding in neatly at the corners (photo 6a), then turn the clutch over. Fold the binding over twice (photo 6b) and secure with a small hand running stitch (photo 6c).

7. On the inside of the flap, at the centre of the curved edge just below the binding, sew on one side of a large press stud. Fold the flap down again, determine where the other side of the press stud should be positioned to correspond, and sew it in place.

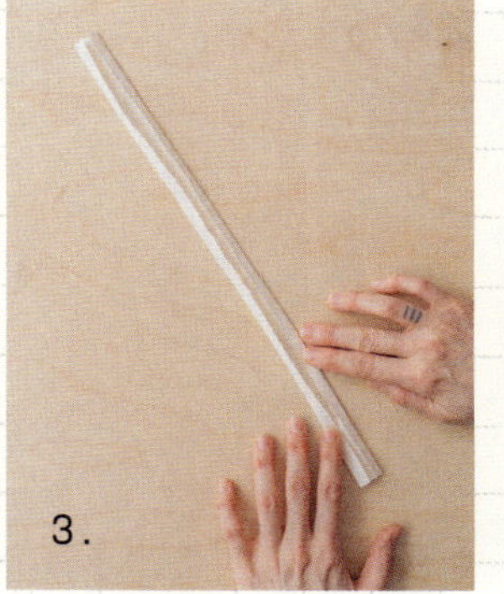
3.

4.

5.

6a.

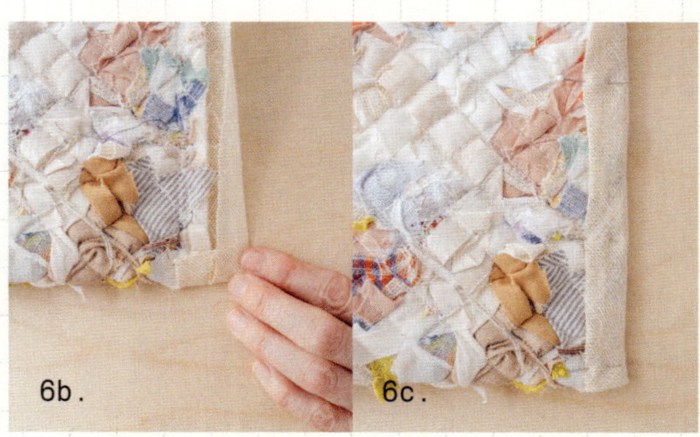
6b.
6c.

7.

INDEX

T

V

W

Z

ACKNOWLEDGEMENTS

Firstly, we would like to thank the team from Quadrille for being so supportive throughout this whole process. Oreolu, Emily, Sarah and Kat, you have made this such a fantastic experience and we have felt so blessed to have your full trust with our vision for this book. We would like to thank all of the gorgeous models who showed up for us – Shoko, Ludjero, Sarah, Anti, Edith and Anna. Thank you to Jessica for being so easy to work with and for taking the most amazing photographs of our clothes and to Amelie for doing a brilliant job with hair and make-up.

We would also like to thank our studio apprentice Katarina for being such an amazing help in the studio during this time, and Josefin for helping us get our paper patterns digitized and graded. Thank you to Symaskinskungen in Malmö, Sweden, for kindly lending us two brilliant sewing machines to use for the book, a PFAFF Passport 3.0 and a PFAFF Coverlock 3.0. A big thanks to Birgitta's dad Karl for always being on call to look after the kids – it really takes a village! We would also like to thank our daughters Astrid and Aila for being super rad and always (almost always) being patient when we have had to bring some extra work home. And finally, thanks to all our friends and family for always being on call to chat and run ideas by!

ABOUT THE AUTHORS

Birgitta Helmersson is a Swedish-Australian designer and pattern maker with over 20 years' experience in fashion and textiles. She launched her self-titled brand in 2013 in Melbourne, Australia, before relocating to Malmö, Sweden, in 2018, where she co-founded Helgrose. She is known for her innovative approach to zero-waste pattern cutting, as well as incorporating craft-based methods to create clothing and textiles from fabric offcuts and repurposed second-hand and vintage materials. Alongside her design work, she has led workshops and lectures on sustainable fashion and zero-waste design in Sweden and internationally. She is the author of *Zero Waste Patterns* (Quadrille, 2023).

Sam Grose is a maker and photographer with a background in the culinary world. Originally a chef by trade, he worked in kitchens around the world before shifting his creative focus to textiles and design. His experience in food informs his approach to making – rooted in resourcefulness, craftsmanship and an appreciation for process-driven work. Originally from the Mornington Peninsula in Australia, he co-founded Helgrose in 2018. Sam has worked extensively with craft-based textile techniques and natural dyeing using food waste and organic materials. As the in-house photographer for his shared businesses, he brings a unique perspective to textile creation, sustainability and visual storytelling.

Sam and Birgitta live in Malmö, Sweden, with their two daughters. Together, they run The Cloth Lab, a creative hub dedicated to sustainability, which houses their in-house brands, Helgrose and Birgitta Helmersson Studio. Focused on upcycling, repurposing and zero-waste techniques, they offer workshops, books, sewing patterns, fabrics, clothing and home furnishings – all designed with their core philosophy in mind: Making Without Waste.

To learn more visit:

www.theclothlab.com

@_theclothlab_

www.helgrose.com

@helgrose

www.birgittahelmersson.com

@birgittahelmersson

Quadrille, Penguin Random House UK,
One Embassy Gardens, 8 Viaduct Gardens,
London SW11 7BW

Quadrille Publishing Limited is part of the Penguin Random House group of companies whose addresses can be found at global.penguinrandomhouse.com

Published by Quadrille in 2025

www.penguin.co.uk

A CIP catalogue record for this book is available from the British Library

ISBN 978 1 83783 3467

10 9 8 7 6 5 4 3 2 1

Managing Director Sarah Lavelle
Editorial Director Harriet Butt
Project Editor Sarah Hoggett
Assistant Editor Oreolu Grillo
Design and Art Direction Emily Lapworth
Photographer Jessica Sidenros
Hair and Make up Amelie Holmberg
Models Anti, Anna, Edith, Ludjero, Sarah, Shoko
Production Director Stephen Lang
Production Controller Sumayyah Waheed

Colour reproduction by F1

Printed in China by C&C Offset Printing Co., Ltd

The authorized representative in the EEA is Penguin Random House Ireland, Morrison Chambers, 32 Nassau Street, Dublin D02 YH68.

Penguin Random House is committed to a sustainable future for our business, our readers and our planet. This book is made from Forest Stewardship Council® certified paper.